STRIFE AND PROGRESS

STRIFE AND PROGRESS

Portfolio Strategies for Managing Urban Schools

Paul T. Hill
Christine Campbell
Betheny Gross

BROOKINGS INSTITUTION PRESS
Washington, D.C.

ABOUT BROOKINGS

The Brookings Institution is a private nonprofit organization devoted to research, education, and publication on important issues of domestic and foreign policy. Its principal purpose is to bring the highest quality independent research and analysis to bear on current and emerging policy problems. Interpretations or conclusions in Brookings publications should be understood to be solely those of the authors.

Copyright © 2013
THE BROOKINGS INSTITUTION
1775 Massachusetts Avenue, N.W., Washington, D.C. 20036
www.brookings.edu

Library of Congress Cataloging-in-Publication data are available
ISBN: 978-0-8157-2427-8 (pbk. : alk. paper)

9 8 7 6 5 4 3 2 1

Printed on acid-free paper

Typeset in Sabon and Strayhorn

Composition by R. Lynn Rivenbark
Macon, Georgia

Printed by R. R. Donnelley
Harrisonburg, Virginia

Contents

Acknowledgments

The people we most need to thank for help with this book are the hundreds who let us interview them or who took part in focus groups. Since we promised anonymity, we can't name them, but they know who they are. They include school district and city officials, business and union leaders, principals, local journalists, foundation staff, and heads of parent, teacher, and community groups in all the cities we studied.

We can name and thank those who contributed ideas and criticism of the work, starting with Michele Cahill, Robin Lake, Sarah Yatsko, Shannon Murtaugh, Jeffrey Henig, Jennifer O'Day, David Menefee-Libey, Mary Vaiana, James Harvey, Sam Sperry, Bruno Manno, Robert Reichardt, Paul Teske, Patrick Murphy, Deb Britt, and Libuse Binder. None of these generous commentators misled us in any way. Any errors or misinterpretations are ours alone.

CHAPTER ONE

Introduction

Yolanda (not an individual but a composite) is a fourteen-year-old girl who attends a New Orleans charter school. She was eight in 2005, just about to enter third grade, when Hurricane Katrina forced her family to flee the city and separate in order to live with relatives. She spent several months out of school but eventually enrolled in elementary school in the small town in Texas where her mother's sister lived.

Schools in the Texas district were not considered at all advanced, so teachers in her new school were surprised to find out how far behind the other students Yolanda was. After trying placement in second grade, they returned her to a third-grade classroom but provided as much extra tutoring as they could.

Her father's work experience helped him get a job with a new construction company in New Orleans in early 2007, so her family was able to reunite and return to the city. Though the house the family had rented before the hurricane was destroyed, the family was able to rent a unit only a mile away. After a few weeks of moving and repairing a rental duplex that was not as "renovated" as promised, her parents contacted the Recovery School District and arranged for Yolanda's placement as a fifth grader in a new K–8 charter school.

The new school is run by a combination of New Orleans business people, college administrators, former New Orleans teachers, and teachers recruited from outside the state. It serves students like Yolanda, many of whom have experienced interrupted education, family separation, and loss of their old home. Moreover, most had been performing well below grade level in the schools they attended before the hurricane.

Throughout this book, we return to Yolanda's story and those of children, parents, and teachers in other cities. In the meantime, a debate rages about whether it is fair for Americans to demand more of their public schools. One side argues that high dropout rates and low achievement, especially among poor and minority students, are rooted in poverty and social conditions that schooling cannot overcome. The other side argues that schools do far less for poor and minority children than they could if they made better use of the time, money, and talent available to them. The debate has become nasty, with the first side claiming that schools and educators are being blamed for society's failings, and the second claiming that teachers unions and other defenders of the status quo put their own interests before those of children.

As is usual in polarized debates, both sides ignore inconvenient facts. Some schools are making innovative uses of time, money, and teaching methods and are having dramatic success with children who are otherwise likely to fail. However, even the most effective schools for disadvantaged children still don't work for all at-risk students. In particular, no one has found a way to reach the small minority of students who do not attend school faithfully and do not do the assigned work. Thus neither side's claims fit all the facts. In their candid moments, debaters on both sides concede both that poverty impedes many students and that many schools serving the poor are poorly staffed and inefficient. But neither side is about to abandon the debate, fearing that the other side would, if left unopposed, either totally dismantle public education or block reasonable efforts to improve it.

We are writing this book because we believe that both sides are partly right and that the current stalemate is harmful to everyone. It is possible both to maintain the core values of public education—including public oversight, a commitment to equity, and fair treatment of educators—and to organize public education so that it is always open to new ideas and new sources of talent. Stalemate leaves Americans in the worst possible position: millions of children leaving school unprepared to be effective participants in a competitive global economy and an increasingly complex political system.

Our goal is to explain a strategy that is emerging in many big cities. The strategy would preserve public education by transforming it from a stagnant entity that cannot adapt to the needs of its students into a

TABLE 1-1. **Financial and School District Portfolios**

Financial portfolio	School district portfolio
Diverse investments	New and promising school options
Constant review of performance	Sophisticated accountability systems
Strategic investment and divestment	Expand successful programs, intervene in or close unsuccessful programs

dynamic public enterprise engaged in a constant search for the set of schools and instructional experiences that best meet the needs of a diverse urban student population.

The Portfolio Strategy: What It Is and What It Isn't

The portfolio strategy, often introduced by mayors and others concerned with a city's future viability, is so named because it is founded on an idea similar to a financial portfolio (table 1-1). A financial manager aims for a diverse portfolio that performs well. She avoids betting everything on one investment, knowing that some holdings will perform much better than expected and some much worse. This manager is agnostic as to which companies are represented but knows that diversity is key and regularly reviews performance as well as industry and company news. When some stocks make impressive gains, more of those are added, and when some are trending poorly, those are sold.

A school district portfolio manager thinks the same way. No school model is right for every child, so the district needs a diverse array of schools. By constantly reviewing school and student outcomes, as well as school climate and neighborhood need, the portfolio manager knows which schools are both performing and trending well, which schools have the possibility of improving, and which schools must be replaced with options that are right for the affected students. Portfolio district managers also track performance closely and make sure everyone in the system has access to good data. The portfolio strategy is a way to seek a solution to a problem that has never been solved before, akin to the methods used to discover remedies to previously incurable illnesses or to develop computers that can do things previously thought impossible. In K–12 education the problem to be solved is how to effectively educate all the children in a large city, including those from the most disadvantaged homes. The portfolio strategy does not assume that the best methods known today will always be the best available. Instead, it incorporates a spirit of continuous improvement, always asking, "Is this the very best we can do for our community's children?"

Not every effort to create a new school or improve an existing one can work as planned the first time. With a portfolio, leaders add more of what's working, eliminate what is not working, assess, and repeat. They also track performance closely and make sure everyone in the system has access to good data. As this book shows, school districts pioneering the use of the portfolio strategy have stirred up serious opposition. People whose jobs will change, or whose positions of influence are put at risk, often oppose the strategy. So do some families and property owners who like their current schools and do not want them to change, even when faced with evidence that some students are not doing well in them.

Ironically, despite the opposition it stirs up, the portfolio strategy has proven more sustainable than more narrowly conceived districtwide programs. As subsequent chapters show, school district portfolio strategies used in such big cities as New York, Washington, Denver, New Orleans, Los Angeles, Chicago, and Hartford have survived the departure of the public officials who introduced them. This rarely happens with narrow districtwide programs, which are identified with strong superintendents and have shallow support. Portfolio strategies can be more sustainable because they remake public education into a civic initiative that is open to both community input and resources.

Why Tell the Portfolio Story?

Our goal in this book is to inform mayors, governors, parents, educators, and civic leaders about the school district portfolio strategy—what it means, how it can be introduced into a city and used to benefit children, what conflicts it creates, and what political and financial resources are necessary to make it work. We think that many readers will conclude that the school district portfolio strategy is sensible, is necessary, can succeed, and is worth the effort.

We do not hide the risks and costs. These are real, as in any great undertaking that opens up new possibilities. Nor do we make claims that every school district that has tried a portfolio strategy has seen all its schools transformed. Though there is positive evidence in terms of school quality and benefits to students, leaders in all the cities we studied are still searching for ways to make their worst schools better and their mediocre schools good.

If the only definition of success is brilliant performance in all things, no city's public schools have attained it. Critics who claim that the strategy is unproven are right, in the same sense that any evidence-based process (like the search for the cure for a disease) is unproven until its success is total. Where critics go wrong is to suggest that the lack of total success to date means that the portfolio strategy should be abandoned in favor of some districtwide programs like class-size reduction.

Unlike traditional districtwide programs, which require total commitment to one idea until it is proven not to work as hoped, the portfolio is adaptable (like a good financial strategy) and lets city leaders hedge their bets. It can't promise success instantly or every time, but its ceiling—what can be accomplished over a long period of continuous improvement—is likely to be higher than that of any single districtwide program. This is because the portfolio strategy is not committed to a single idea about how to improve schools. It allows school districts to try out many ideas in a disciplined way, use common metrics to compare different initiatives, build on what works best, and keep searching for something better.

The need for effective public education is greater than ever. As lifetime jobs disappear, workers are forced to compete with motivated and educated people from around the world; effective citizenship requires literacy and critical thinking; and consumers must be wary and informed. This is also a time when public education must compete with many other demands for public funding and can't expect dramatic increases in resources. In this situation there is no choice but to seek promising ideas from wherever they are available. That is the essence of the portfolio strategy and, we think, the future course of public education.

This book explains the portfolio strategy in detail: how it works, what it accomplishes, and how it handles (or exacerbates) the conflicts of public education. Though we try to present a balanced appraisal of the portfolio strategy, we do take one definite position: that the conflict stirred up by a reform strategy is in itself not evidence of its failure or a reason not to try it. Any change intended to drastically improve the performance of schools is bound to stir up these conflicts in some way; the fact that conflicts are raging now is evidence only that real changes are made, not that the changes themselves are good or bad.

Our Research

Our findings are based on a thirty-month study conducted by the Center on Reinventing Public Education with support from the Carnegie Corporation of New York. The study consisted of extensive case studies of five cities—New York, New Orleans, Washington, Chicago, and Denver—that had transformed either all or major parts of their school districts via the portfolio strategy. We visited each of the cities several times, starting in January 2009, interviewing key actors in the city and school systems, interest groups in favor or opposed to the strategy (including union leaders), philanthropists, and educators. We also closely tracked developments in the implementation strategy (including major changes in direction and leadership) and gathered outcomes data (including analyses of student achievement and changes in teacher quality).

Thanks to the Annie E. Casey Foundation we were able to add case studies from Hartford and Baltimore, which provided a perspective on how the strategy can be implemented in smaller cities. Starting in late 2011 we were able to make a close study of Cleveland, which had just committed to a portfolio strategy under the leadership of Mayor Frank Jackson.

Chapters to Come

Chapter 2 summarizes the results of our close examination of school districts using the portfolio strategy over three years. It identifies the many attributes these districts have in common, such as adopting performance-based accountability systems for all schools, establishing a financially level playing field between existing and new schools, working to make themselves attractive to new principals and school leaders, opening themselves up to civic and human resources previously excluded from schools, closing unproductive schools and replacing them with more productive new schools, starting new schools, and making sure schools have choices about where they purchase teacher enhancement programs and other services. The chapter also shows how these districts differ, both in the overall design of their strategies and the degree to which their strategies have been implemented.

Chapter 3 tells stories of how portfolio strategies emerged. It focuses on two cities, New York and Denver, with very different histories and politics. In New York, the takeover of schools by an extremely powerful mayor led to adoption of the portfolio strategy; moreover, Chancellor Joel Klein was able to exercise a tremendous degree of discretion, recruiting a small working group of highly capable outsiders to turn the school district around. In Denver, Superintendents Michael Bennet and Tom Boasberg shared Klein's ideas about the need to break up the public school monopoly but were constrained by the need to maintain a shaky majority on an elected conventional school board. Comparison of New York and Denver (with some further examples from Chicago, Washington, New Orleans, Hartford, Cleveland, and Baltimore) illustrates both how portfolio strategies can emerge under very different political circumstances and what preconditions school districts using a portfolio strategy have in common.

Chapter 4 examines the topic that is so often associated with portfolio strategies: conflict. It shows why there is always potential for strife around the subject of public education. Parents, teachers, neighbors, elected officials, and taxpayers all have their own interests, which overlap only imperfectly and partially with those of children. Those parties can act in ways they think are consistent with children's interests, yet clash with one another. The chapter shows how city leaders and others concerned about public education have handled these conflicts and how—or if—they have been resolved. Portfolio strategies have reopened issues that had for a long time been decisively settled in favor of one group over another. By doing so, the strategy raises the possibility that previously neglected groups could get a better deal. Only time will tell whether that, or some other less desirable result, will emerge.

The fifth chapter asks the bottom-line question: whether or not children benefit from a portfolio strategy. It first lays out an approach to assessing effects on different groups of students: those whom the strategy allowed to enroll in new schools, those who were forced to leave schools that were closed, and those whose existing schools experienced new performance pressures and the need to compete for students. Though no city now has all the data required to fully assess its portfolio strategy, this chapter assembles evidence from many sources to make the first broad outcomes assessment. No reader will be surprised to learn that the results are mixed. But there is evidence that the portfolio strategy has succeeded in creating new options for the most disadvantaged students.

Chapter 6 assesses the future of the portfolio strategy as the leaders who first introduced it to their cities leave the scene. The chapter starts with a surprising result: that portfolio strategies have survived and even flourished despite the departure of figures like Joel Klein in New York City, Michelle Rhee in Washington, Paul Vallas in New Orleans, Michael Bennet in Denver, Arne Duncan in Chicago, Stephen Adamowski in Hartford, and Ramon Cortines in Los Angeles. Except for Klein and Duncan, successors were hired expressly to advance the portfolio strategy, and many have done so aggressively. In New York and Chicago, the strategy is back, but its future depends on city politics and superintendent succession.

These conclusions might be surprising in light of the phenomenon of "churn" identified by Rick Hess, who observes that, in general, school district reform strategies last only as long as the superintendent who adopts them.[1] They become dead letters sometime late in the originating superintendent's term, as the enthusiasm surrounding his or her initial hiring evaporates, and they are replaced by something different when the next superintendent takes office. We consider two possible explanations for the hardiness of portfolio strategies, one based on widespread support for the idea in the business and professional communities and one based on the development of strong leadership "benches" within districts using the strategy (henceforth called portfolio districts). We also suggest the ways that federal and state policy can make the portfolio strategy a practical option for other communities that want to try it.

Chapter 7 discusses the likely future of the portfolio strategy, particularly whether, once a school district has adopted it, the district can ever go back to the old bureaucracy-dominated system of public education. We conclude that the portfolio strategy will have a "ratchet" effect, subject to occasional pauses but not to reversal.

The portfolio strategy is a complex response to a messy and multifaceted problem. It responds to a clear need to create new possibilities for children whose futures have been put at risk by weakened, big city, public school systems; but it is also complex and multifaceted, and it will have better results in some places and times than in others.

Yolanda's future, and that of millions of other children in big city schools, depends on the skills and commitment of the adults in her community, including teachers, district leaders, elected officials, and interest advocates. A portfolio strategy can enable adults to come together for effective action, but it cannot succeed without commitment, good will, and sustained effort.

CHAPTER TWO
The Portfolio Strategy in Practice

While Yolanda was just settling into her temporary home in Texas, peo-
ple in the Louisiana state capitol, Baton Rouge, were worried about the
time when she and thousands of others might return to New Orleans. The
vast majority of school buildings in New Orleans were uninhabitable; the
city's Ninth Ward and many other smaller neighborhoods were totally
destroyed. Like the children, educators were also dispersed across the
whole country, and many might never return.

State Superintendent Cecil Picard was determined to have schools be
open whenever the children arrived. But he was not sure who would
come back, when, where they would live, or what kinds or remediation
they would need. Picard and other officials, including Democratic gover-
nor Kathleen Blanco, decided to deal with these uncertainties via the port-
folio strategy. The state would offer schools using different combinations
of instruction and support for students, hoping to find the right match for
every student. Schools would not be permanent, but changeable, depend-
ing on performance and student need. The state would use chartering to
create schools that could be easily closed if they were not needed or if they
didn't match the needs of the children returning to New Orleans.

The portfolio strategy is a new approach to the way a city provides public education. The people responsible for public education—the local
superintendent or school board or, in some cases, the mayor—continually
search for new models of schooling and innovative approaches to instruction that might get better results than current schools. School districts,
which once operated schools bureaucratically, are transformed into per-

formance managers. Performance managers don't control schools by regulation. Instead, they create freedom of action for school leaders and teachers, track and compare schools' performance, and try to expand the numbers of high-performing schools and reduce the number of low-performing ones. The portfolio strategy is built to create high-quality schools regardless of provider, giving schools autonomy over staff and funding, and holding all schools accountable for performance.

Portfolio School Districts in 2012

The first count, in 2008, of portfolio school districts—those that exhibited some or many of the characteristics of the portfolio strategy—put the number at four: New York City, New Orleans Recovery School District (RSD), Chicago, and Washington. In 2012 it was used in almost thirty districts across the country, including early adopters such as New York City and New Orleans, smaller districts such as Hartford, Baltimore, and Cleveland, and western cities such as Denver, Los Angeles, Oakland, and Sacramento (figure 2-1).[1]

As used in these districts the portfolio strategy is a method of problem solving, not a program that can be bolted down and expected to work automatically.

As used in these districts the portfolio strategy is a method of problem solving, not a program that can be bolted down and expected to work automatically. Instead, leaders pursuing the portfolio strategy identify neighborhoods and groups of children who lack good schooling options and find ways to create better alternatives. These innovations can include asking outstanding principals and teachers to create new schools and chartering schools to groups with good track records. It can also include forming partnerships with city agencies, colleges, private schools, and businesses that can help enhance schools' instructional and student support programs.

Districts pursuing the portfolio strategy are indifferent about who runs a school (whether the district, a charter operator, or some other entity); but they seek continuous improvement, both in individual schools and in the city's overall supply of public schools. However, the portfolio strategy is more than just an opening and closing strategy. While those actions generate a lot of attention, the portfolio district is probably most involved

FIGURE 2-1. Portfolio School Districts in the United States, 2012

in working to improve the environment for schools that are already good while also creating opportunities and pressure for them to become better.

The portfolio strategy seeks to transform a city where many of the ablest teachers and principals have been reluctant to work into a magnet for talent. This can entail experimenting with new methods of teacher recruitment and compensation, with ways to allow scientists, artists, and other experts to teach in the schools, and with new professional development approaches designed to improve whole schools, not just individual teachers.

It is important to note that not all of these approaches work as planned the first time. With the portfolio strategy, leaders add more of what's working, eliminate what is not working, assess, and repeat. They also track performance closely and make sure everyone in the system has access to good data.

Portfolio Strategies and Student Needs

Despite decades of reform, America still does not know how to provide effective schools for millions of underserved students. Half of all low-income, immigrant, and minority children never earn a regular high school diploma. In many cities, more than 30 percent of all low-income African American students score below the bottom 10th percentile on national reading and math tests.[2]

It is not just low-income children who are not succeeding. The nation's graduation rate hovers at 68 percent. Only 25 percent of high school graduates meet college readiness benchmarks.[3] Even America's best students are

FIGURE 2-2. Ingredients for Continuous Improvement in Education

Autonomy, data, new support

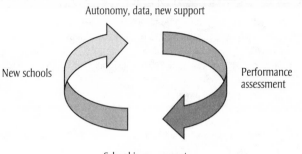

New schools

Performance
assessment

School improvement

not rising to the top internationally.[4] These realities demand new approaches that allow for different types of schools that are free to innovate and meet students' unique needs. Traditional school districts were designed with the opposite purpose in mind: to oversee a one-best-system of schooling. The portfolio school district approach is one way to rebuild school districts to support and oversee a differentiated system of schools.

Different localities have adopted the portfolio idea in slightly different ways. New York and New Orleans have adopted the idea citywide, so that all schools have the same freedoms and performance-based accountability, while Chicago and Washington initially adopted the idea only in part.

Most portfolio districts start with the same objective: ensuring that no child attends a school in which he or she is not likely to learn. Leading portfolio districts like New York City, New Orleans, and Denver support existing schools that are succeeding with the children they serve, close unproductive schools, create new ones similar to schools that have already proven effective, and seek even more effective models. To identify unproductive schools, and also to help parents and administrators identify the kinds of schools that ought to be made available to as many students as possible, the districts have worked to build data systems that would allow assessment of schools by measuring the amount of learning attained each year by their students.

These actions, working together as in figure 2-2, are the core of the portfolio idea. The district seeks continuous improvement by providing the autonomy, data, and new sources of support, then assessing the performance of all schools, closing the lowest performing schools, and creating new opportunities for students who have been in the least productive schools.

BOX 2-1.   **Seven Components of a Portfolio Strategy**

The portfolio strategy is a performance management model for districts that aim to create dramatic student achievement gains at scale. It centers on creating more high-quality schools regardless of provider, giving schools autonomy over staff and funding, and holding all schools accountable for performance. The portfolio strategy is built on seven key components.

Component 1: Good options and choices for all families

   Opening of new schools based on parent/student/neighborhood need

   Opening of new schools with outside operators (such as charters)

   School choice for all families

   Coordination of enrollment and school information for families across sectors

   Aggressive recruitment of external new school providers

   Intentional development of internal new school providers

   Equity and access to charter and nontraditional schools for special education students and English language learners

Component 2: School autonomy

   Universal autonomy: all schools control staff selection and deselection, budget, pay, and curriculum choice

   Freedom to seek waivers on contracts regarding use of time, teacher resources, and student grouping

(continued)

This process continues indefinitely, so that the district is progressively less tolerant of unproductive schools. Schools—new and old—that were once considered "good enough" will ultimately experience pressure for continuous improvement.[5]

Seven Components of the Portfolio Strategy

None of the actions listed in box 2-1 is unique to portfolio districts. States and localities have been opening new schools from time to time, assessing school performance, and closing schools that lost enrollment or tolerated chaotic environments in which students could not learn. What is new in portfolio districts is the determination to make these actions complement one another and to adopt the continuous improvement process as the district's core strategy. Closing schools accomplishes little unless it is linked

BOX 2-1. Seven Components of a Portfolio Strategy (Continued)

Component 3: Pupil-based funding for all schools

Pupil-based funding

High proportion of district funds being sent to schools

Common pricing of facilities and services across sectors

School-level flexibility to pay for new models of teaching and organization (such as blended learning models)

Plan in place for low-enrollment schools that cannot survive on pupil-based funding (such as planned closure and providing extra funding to see current cohort of students finish)

Component 4: Talent-seeking strategy

Recruitment of new principals and teachers to the district

Intensive development of strong teachers and leaders from within the district

Policies in place for using alternative pipelines to find and develop talent

Performance-based teacher retention

Contractual arrangements in place that free up schools to have performance-based teacher pay

Component 5: Sources of support for schools

Schools free to choose support from diverse independent providers

Strategy to intentionally attract and support diverse independent providers

Component 6: Performance-based accountability for schools

Data systems that allow measurement of annual student growth

Accountability systems that compare schools on student growth, climate, and improvement

Rich information systems to guide school self-assessment and planning

Common student performance standards for all schools

Publication of a school report card

Closure of persistently low-performing district and charter schools

Component 7: Extensive public engagement

Communication plan to convey information about reform strategy and progress (including need for school closures)

Public criteria and schedule for school closings and openings

Feedback loop for parents and community members to express concerns and receive responses

Partnerships and coalitions with key stakeholders

to a strategy for creating new options for children and neighborhoods that have been poorly served, and both those actions need to be informed by real performance data, not just by hunches, opportunity, and political calculation.

In applying the portfolio idea to their entire districts, leaders in early adopting cities such as New York and New Orleans quickly learned that the four core actions (opening, authority, closing, using data) are necessary but not sufficient. Other actions must be taken and capacities developed to supplement these. Working from different contexts, districts have learned that a complete portfolio strategy has the same seven key components.

Many school districts face continued low student performance despite serious attempts and investments to boost it. Portfolio districts have come to the conclusion that continuing to provide the same set of schools will not yield the dramatic improvements they seek. They decide that a centralized, one-size-fits-all approach is not working and that strong school leaders are the best people to make the call on what their students need— the curriculum, instruction, class size, culture, and so on. That leads them to give principals autonomy. They also decide they need people who can both try new approaches yet can live with performance accountability: any initiative no matter how well intentioned will be abandoned if it does not work for students. This leads portfolio leaders to develop a talent-seeking strategy, to bring in skilled, creative educators with the belief that every child can succeed given the right tools and support.

These components reinforce one another:

—Choice is meaningful only if schools are autonomous—that is, they can make specific promises about what students will experience and learn; that means they must have autonomy—for example, they control their own workforces and schedules.

—City and school leaders must attract and keep talented people who can make autonomous schools work.

—Schools must all be resourced equitably, with equal or weighted amounts of money available to pay for a student's education, no matter what school she attends, so schools can compete on a financially level playing field.

—Autonomous schools still need multiple sources of support: access to data, advice, and instructional materials relevant to their own specific situations.

With freedom of action, equitable funding, access to skilled help, and a rich talent pool, schools can fairly be held accountable for performance. City and district leaders can be confident that all schools have a chance to succeed. Even when those attributes of the portfolio strategy are in place, it can fail if parents, teachers, and voters don't understand what is being done and why. Thus leaders of portfolio strategies must engage families, educators, and the general public so that all can understand the strategy and have reason to believe it is being implemented competently and fairly.

Though there is a logical order to the seven components presented in box 2-1, cities have differed on where they start and how thoroughly they develop the components of the portfolio strategy. The following discussion explains what we found about how the different cities have implemented the strategy and what elements are still under development in particular places.

Good Options and Choices for All Families

Family choice among schools is a necessary starting place for any district that believes no child should attend a school in which he or she is not likely to learn. Portfolio districts approach choice in two ways, via student assignment policies and by opening new schools.

New Student Assignments. Portfolio district leaders urge families to consider schools known to be productive, but they try to avoid mandating school assignments. Because many of the new schools developed by a portfolio district are designed for particular purposes—to follow an instructional theory, create a definite student culture, or offer special kinds of student support—district leaders need to think about student assignment systems that give students and families choices about where they go to school.

Like many aspects of the portfolio strategy, a workable and fair student assignment system is not easy to build, especially at the outset. Productive and unproductive schools are unevenly distributed across the district, and some neighborhoods have few high-quality options. By allowing families to opt out of these schools, some schools will be underenrolled. Identifying weak schools is the beginning of a multistep process, which includes determining whether less-productive schools can improve rapidly, closing the least promising ones, and opening new schools in underserved areas.

Figuring out student assignment through choice is a complicated process. New York City is a good example of how some districts are developing systems to manage the continuing challenge of student assignment

---

BOX 2-2. **Admissions Lotteries, New York City High School**

"In 2004, NYC DOE school officials launched a new choice process featuring a computerized matching model designed by Harvard economics professor Alvin Roth. Derived from matching markets in medical residencies, kidney donations, sororities, law clerkships, and Internet auctions, the new system requires students to select a dozen schools; the mathematical formula behind the system eliminates waiting lists and the opportunity for favoritism (the school system's computer rather than principals now has the final say on where students go) and greatly increases students' chances of attending schools they've selected.

The number of students attending schools they hadn't chosen plummeted from 35,000 in 2003 to 790 in 2009. This past spring, more than 65,000 of the city's rising ninth graders were granted one of their top five choices for 2011–12, and after the completion of a supplemental-selection round, only a small fraction had to be administratively placed because they couldn't be matched with schools they wanted."

Source: "NYC Program Means Real Public School Choice," *Education Week*, August 19, 2011.

---

in a portfolio district. New York City holds all admissions lotteries at the same time, so that no school can gain an advantage by "jumping the gun," and places all students simultaneously, so that everyone has a known chance of gaining admission to the most popular schools. In 2011 Denver and New Orleans adopted similar strategies, which coordinated student enrollment procedures across traditional public schools and charter schools. In Denver that has meant the elimination of over seventy application forms that parents had to navigate for particular schools on different deadlines. They were replaced with one common form, due on one date, regardless of where or what kind of school a parent is choosing.

Improvements in Existing Schools. Although they might be attracted to charter schools and other totally new starts, portfolio district leaders in cities other than New Orleans understand that the majority of a city's students, teachers, and parents are to be found in existing schools. Portfolio district leaders continue to support excellent existing schools and try to create circumstances under which other existing schools can improve. Closing existing schools and opening new ones are options on the margin, but outcomes for most students depend on the performance of existing schools.

Fair funding and sophisticated student enrollment systems give existing schools a chance to compete with new schools for students. However, early in the implementation of portfolio strategies, badly managed enrollment processes led to some schools being overwhelmed with challenging students and inattentive parents. The new admissions processes described above are meant to protect existing schools from being overburdened.

Though not all incumbent teachers and principals have welcomed the combination of autonomy and performance pressure that the portfolio strategy brings, many of the performance gains on which reform leaders hang their hats—in New York, Denver, Chicago, Washington, Hartford, and Baltimore—come from existing schools making use of new autonomies in staffing and budget.

In one aggressive effort to improve existing schools, New York City initiated an innovation zone (iZone), in which existing district-run and charter schools could experiment with new partnerships with independent support organizations and new uses of technology to increase student learning time and teacher productivity.[6] This initiative, which by 2012 included more than 250 existing schools, is projected to expand to as many as a third of all of New York City's 1,700 public schools by 2014. Although no other city has taken so ambitious an approach to innovation of their existing schools, Denver and Chicago hope to adopt elements of this New York example.

New Schools. Another way to provide choice is to encourage the growth of charter schools. Some state charter school laws allow districts to authorize charter schools, while other districts can only invite potential charter providers by urging them to apply to other authorizers designated by the state. A basic defining element of every portfolio district, however, is the presence of some charter schools. Some districts have encouraged robust growth, with New York City opening over 150 charter schools by fall 2012 (almost 10 percent of district schools).[7] Denver Public Schools sponsors 41 (or 25 percent of district schools), and Chicago authorizes 96 charter schools (almost 15 percent of all of its schools). Almost 80 percent of all New Orleans and 40 percent of all Washington public schools are now charters.[8]

School choice allows districts to attract high-quality school providers to infuse promising school options into neighborhoods that have few high-quality options. While a district works to provide longer term improvements for some of its low-performing schools, it can also offer families immediate access to promising new schools or ones that have a record of achievement in other cities.

Some districts are also offering choice through new district-operated schools. Denver, New York City, and Washington have opened new and distinctive district-run schools, deliberately creating new options and sharpening the focus of these schools to compete for students.

When portfolio district leaders coordinate neighborhood needs and preferences with the creation of new schools, choice also allows the district to better pair school programs with what communities need. If one neighborhood has a high percentage of English language learners, the district can consider opening a dual-language school to attract both English and Spanish speakers. It might consider opening a blended learning school, like California's Rocketship schools, which use individualized computer instruction for learning skills for several hours in the day, thus allowing for much smaller class size when students work with teachers. In another neighborhood, project-based learning—or a STEM (an acronym for science, technology, engineering, and mathematics) school built in collaboration with a university or industry—might be what is missing from the portfolio. In any case, school choice allows districts to create a rich array of high-demand schools, no matter where they are sited, and allows families immediate high-quality options for their children, no matter where they live.

As cities initiate their portfolio strategies, they differ on whether to create new elementary or secondary schools or to create new schools at all levels. New York City started with high schools, driven by evidence that many neighborhood high schools had become dropout factories. The city broke up failing high schools in the Bronx and Manhattan, creating multiple small schools in each existing building. It also built "multiple pathways to graduation" schools, designed to help teenagers who had fallen off the track to graduation regain lost credits. Schools offered differing combinations of remedial instruction, tutoring, flexible schedules for students who had children or needed to work, paired instruction and job experience, and access to online materials.[9] Ten years into its portfolio strategy, however, most of the new openings in New York are at the elementary level.

In contrast, New Orleans emphasized new school creation at the elementary level in the first several years after Hurricane Katrina and is now trying to create new charter high schools to replace several ineffective schools that the Recovery School District (RSD) had tried to run directly. The other cities we studied created new elementary and secondary schools from the outset.

School Autonomy

It may come as a surprise to readers that, in many districts, principals have control over almost nothing. Teachers are hired to work at a school without the principal's consent, and senior teachers from another school can bump incumbent junior teachers if there are layoffs. If a principal has an open teaching position, a teacher without an assignment gets first choice. In addition, principals have little say in hiring their administrative, cafeteria, or janitorial staffs. While they may be given a budget, most everything on it is already allocated to teacher salaries and central office services, such as teacher professional development or building maintenance. In traditional districts, a school of 500 students can have an operating budget in excess of $5 million, but principals have told us that they actually control only $30,000 to $70,000 for field trips, copying, presenters, and so forth.

Before the portfolio strategy introduced greater school autonomy, principals were expected to manage teaching staffs that they did not choose and to make do when teachers had conflicting visions or motivations. Principal preparation and the job itself was geared to instructional leadership only; the district, in effect, would take care of the rest. However, most principals will say that each school has different needs and that the central office's one-size-fits-all decisions rarely work in the best interests of the school and its students. It's little wonder so many principals are frustrated when federal, state, and district accountability systems demand better results from them when they have almost no control over how they spend money, over who teaches the students, or over what curriculum they teach.[10]

In portfolio districts, the principal is the center of the reform. New York City was an early and significant champion of this idea. As chancellor, Joel Klein believed that the most important figure in improving student achievement was the school leader and that leaders should be given as much authority as possible to make the right decisions for their school—getting to choose who was part of their teaching and administrative team and having the budget and freedom to buy the services they felt would support the school. In exchange, principals would need to work within their budget and would be held accountable for results through comparisons to schools like theirs and to the district overall. Applying this to all schools, not just charters, means that existing schools are strengthened, have a greater chance to do what they need to succeed with students, and can be held fairly accountable for performance.

In early 2002 Klein started a pilot of this idea: the relatively small sixty-school Empowerment Zone, a group of early adopting principals who were attracted to these ideas and ready to be held accountable for their work. Over the course of several years, autonomy was eventually shared districtwide. This gave the district time to work with leaders who may not have had strong operational skills. It also gave some principals time to decide to leave.

No other district has made school autonomy as pervasive and complete as New York City. In New Orleans, where the vast majority of schools are charters, these schools have great autonomy, but the remaining RSD-run schools (current count twelve, with numbers declining steadily) do not.

Some districts have expressed hesitation at turning over so much responsibility to principals who may not have experience or training in handling everything from large budgets to hiring to choosing the right curriculum. In Baltimore teacher selection and pay is still controlled by the teacher contract; in Hartford autonomy is limited to the few charters and a group of high-performing schools. Until recent years in Chicago, only charter and specialty schools and a few excellent schools deemed to have "earned" autonomy had control over their budgets and staffing. However, Chicago's mayor, Rahm Emanuel, has pledged to give all Chicago school leaders control over school hiring and staffing. For many cities, limited autonomy may be the best way to start, letting a pilot group of the most ready school leaders be the first cohort, while training and coaching the remaining leaders, with the plan that in three to five years all schools will have autonomy.

Autonomy is important both for principals and districts because it removes the district from the inherent conflict of telling principals what to do and then faulting them whenever schools don't improve. It also gives principals and teachers the freedom to do what they think is right for their individual students, something that is very difficult for central offices to do well from afar.

Pupil-Based Funding

School funding formulas are an important part of putting the portfolio strategy into action. Principals need control of their actual budgets so they can make the best choices for their schools. When families choose where they want their children to go to school, attaching dollars to the children rather than the school allows schools with high demand to expand and schools with low demand to be phased out.

The portfolio strategy places several demands on a school finance system. First, consistent with school autonomy, the strategy demands that school leaders have authority to use money to, for example, extend their school's hours, vary class sizes according to student need and teacher ability, create their own mix of junior and senior teachers, and make trade-offs between staff salaries and instructional technology or purchased services.

Second, the strategy demands that district leaders capture the funds formerly used by a closed school so these funds can be transferred to whatever schools its students next attend. Because a school closing is often not instantaneous—loss of enrollment is one of many signals that a school is spiraling down and should be considered for closure—districts need to avoid paying full administrative and teaching staffs in schools that are being hollowed out of students. This means that schools losing students must also lose staff continually, until such time as they are closed and no longer receive any funds.

Oakland has developed a solution to this. Each year, principals meet with a finance manager to build a budget based on the number of children enrolled in the school. A school that is losing enrollment would realize that it needs to attract more students. If the figures do not improve, the principal would then try to build a leaner program based on per pupil funds. If it looks like too paltry a sum to offer a healthy school experience, the principal would decide whether the school should close. If that were the case, the district would actually increase funds to the school so it could phase out with this year's graduating class. This increase would allow the students a fair schooling experience but would end the subsidizing of a school that because of either shifting demographics or the inability to improve outcomes could not attract enough children.

Pupil-based funding, or ensuring that funds follow the student, means that dollars flow to schools based on enrollment and can be used to pay salaries, other resources, assistance from the central office, and independent providers. As few dollars as possible are held in the central office to pay for oversight functions and new school development.

Former New York City chancellor Klein understood from the beginning that a strategy of closing unproductive schools and creating new ones would not be feasible if great amounts of money were tied up in central office programs, guaranteed jobs, or formal administrative structures. He also wanted to make it possible for school leaders to use money flexibly.

Klein reasoned that the most direct way to accomplish these things was to create a wholly new system for allocating funds, from one based on programs and staffing tables to one based on student enrollment. He introduced the idea of the Empowerment Zone autonomy pilot and applied it districtwide within five years. The districtwide implementation came at the same time as central office expenditures were dramatically cut, so that school leaders could control the lion's share (70 percent) of all funds. Klein wanted to get that number closer to 85 percent.

Other portfolio districts have acknowledged the need for such a change in financing, and the Louisiana Recovery School District has moved rapidly in that direction. Three-quarters of its schools already have direct control over finances, because they are charter schools; per-pupil revenue is funneled directly to them by the district. Hartford has also instituted per-pupil funding. Denver has a pupil-based funding system, though it is constrained by collective bargaining agreement provisions that allow senior (and more expensive) teachers to choose where they will work regardless of budgetary implications.

> *Weighting pupil-base funding to reflect student needs gives schools an incentive to attract challenging students.*

Chicago and Washington acknowledge the advantages of pupil-based funding but have been slow to adopt it—in Chicago because of fear of a backlash from schools that were receiving far more than the districtwide per-pupil average and in Washington because former chancellor Michelle Rhee wanted to spend a great deal extra in particular schools she was personally trying to make over. Under new leadership since 2011, Chicago is moving rapidly toward pupil-based funding.

Another benefit to pupil-based funding occurs when it is weighted to reflect student needs: it becomes an incentive to encourage schools to attract what would otherwise be considered challenging students.

Talent-Seeking Strategy

One of the most prominent and, at times, controversial elements of the portfolio strategy is its focus on the people who lead and teach in schools.

Like many reforms in public education, the portfolio district reform strategy demands a lot of people. It requires teachers and principals who have the capacity and initiative to drive self-directed school improvement in a strong accountability environment and also to attract strong candidates with these qualities. It also requires a remissioned central office, moving away from supporting programs and monitoring compliance to one that exists to serve the school leader and help raise student achievement.

When a district pursues the portfolio strategy, it emphasizes school freedom in hiring; it tries to maximize the quality of choices schools have but doesn't mandatorily assign teachers. To do this, it must be able to negotiate a host of complex relationships, to support and monitor a differentiated system of schools, and to manage the overall performance of their portfolio. Portfolio school district leaders can sometimes find these skills among the people in their existing schools and district offices, but in the past, district staffing systems have often left talent to chance, doing little to seek out high-quality candidates from other districts or the private sector, develop them, and retain them.

RSD leaders in New Orleans sought to attract talented educators from Louisiana and across the country, hoping to normalize an education system that had accepted low performance. State superintendent Paul Pastorek and RSD leader Paul Vallas relied heavily on Teach for America (TFA) and the New Teacher Project to provide new teachers and eventually leaders for new charter schools. They hired former New Orleans teachers in great numbers—but only those who could pass a nationally normed skills test.[11] And they recruited former New Orleans residents who were leading outstanding schools as far away as the United Kingdom to return and start new schools. Though many feared that New Orleans would lose its appeal in the world market for talent and thus suffer a decline in the numbers of TFA volunteers willing to work there, the predicted shortfalls have not occurred.

Early in their efforts, several portfolio school district leaders transformed their staffing systems to better support the performance and flexibility demanded by the portfolio strategy. In both New York City under Chancellor Klein and Washington under Chancellor Rhee, the leaders reimagined the way districts managed human capital from end to end: how they hire, train, place, evaluate, and reward teachers and leaders. Their talent strategy examines how the entire system, not just the district's human resource department, helps or hinders the district's ability to attract and retain the teachers, principals, and central office administrators it needs.

Overall, both districts followed similar courses of action.[12] The chancellors assigned a core member of their top leadership team to manage the talent strategy. These leaders were charged with overseeing policies and practices for the entire employee life cycle: sourcing, development, deployment, performance management, rewarding, and retention. Usually, school districts spread the oversight and management of these functions over various units and offices; as a result, no one has the authority—or accountability—to ensure that all parts of the system work together to support the district's talent needs.

Traditional human resource departments are deeply mired in processing paper—forms, résumés, payroll, and so on. Portfolio districts separate the strategic (for example, how to attract higher caliber leaders) and the transactional (for example, managing payroll and benefits) dimensions of talent management. To ensure that the district performs both sides well, district leaders assign them to different groups. They also borrow from the private sector to improve the basic management processes in human resources (HR)—ensuring, for example, that payroll is accurate and timely and that employee questions about benefits, leave, and other important issues are addressed quickly.

The districts also removed bottlenecks to speed up staffing processes to help the right people with the right skills get to the right places. For example, New York City renegotiated its teacher contract to give principals more control over teacher hiring, curtailing seniority privileges, ending the "bumping" of junior teachers, and requiring "excessed" teachers (those who lose their positions for a variety of reasons, including enrollment declines or school closures) to apply for vacancies instead of being assigned to them. The ending of forced placement and bumping—along with a transfer plan that allows any teacher to transfer without regard to seniority—has resulted in a system that gives the principal the ability to hire who they believe to be the best candidate to teach in their schools, advancing the philosophy of the principal as the locus of control.

In addition to rethinking teacher contracts, the districts also examined ways to make certification rules more flexible.[13] In Washington district leaders revised certification rules so they could expand their pool of teacher applicants to include selective partnerships with outside talent providers. For classroom teachers, these groups include well-known organizations, such as Teach For America and the New Teacher Project, which help support city-specific teaching fellows programs. For principals, they include city-based leadership academies, such as the New York City Leadership Academy, that tap and develop leadership talent inside the district, as well as national groups like New Leaders.

Alternative talent providers give districts greater access to a wider pool of nontraditional, entrepreneurial teachers and leaders than traditional certification routes and, especially with regard to school leadership, populate schools with people whose skills are aligned with the reform agenda.

Although district leaders look outside for new types of teachers and principals, they do not see them as the only answer to their HR needs. Outside talent providers cannot, for example, be relied upon to provide enough candidates to address all of the district's hiring needs, and sometimes districts seek more experience than these programs can offer. One strategy used by Washington is to search almost exclusively for experienced principals with proven records of urban school success, rather than invest several years in getting new principals up to speed.

Districts pursuing the portfolio strategy are also redesigning hiring, evaluation, and compensation policies and practices to focus more on performance. In New York City, for example, the district has revised its principal selection protocols to include a wider array of performance assessments and work samples, including having candidates provide a writing sample, evaluate a complicated piece of data in front of judges (a budget, a student achievement problem, or crisis in the school), and evaluate a videotape of a teacher conducting a lesson. The district has also worked with leadership training institutions, including colleges of education, to adopt the district's "leadership competencies" into their preparation and development programs. New York City requires teacher candidates to submit a writing sample and has created a candidate quality index to assist principals who are seeking new teachers for positions in their schools.

Across both districts and in Denver, leaders revised their principal and teacher compensation systems to include financial rewards for performance.[14] In New York City, for example, principals are eligible for an annual bonus of up to $25,000 based on student achievement results. Leaders in Washington revised their evaluation systems so that they help identify and recognize differences in performance, rather than provide everyone with a "satisfactory" rating. Teachers can earn bonuses (in the range of $10,000 to $25,000) for receiving good evaluations. In 2011, 670 teachers were eligible for this bonus.[15] Similarly, in New Orleans, RSD leaders encouraged effective young teachers to become charter school leaders years before they would have been considered eligible in a conventional school district. This opportunity, and the possibility of making a principal's salary after only a few years of teaching, kept many people in New Orleans who had been recruited from other places.

New York and Washington also worked to change the culture of the central office to focus on performance. Incumbent HR staff members were required to "reapply" for their positions, and in many cases new staff were hired who fit a new emphasis on customer service and accountability.

New York, Washington, Baltimore, and Chicago under former superintendent Ron Huberman also tried to change the culture in the central office through the use of new performance metrics and accountability tools for central office personnel. In Washington, for example, top district managers have weekly reviews with the district's executive management team to go over their goals and progress (called SchoolStat, modeled after New York City's Crimestat). For HR this means reviewing a host of metrics, such as the number of vacancies in each school and across the system, recruitment and application trends, and the quality of customer service calls (for example, duration to solution and outcome of inquiries). The fact that many central office employees came to call this process "slaughterstat" is evidence of how profoundly it challenged the preexisting central office culture.

It is hard to say how this combination of people, training, and accountability systems is changing the way people work in these districts, but practice seems to be shifting. Before adopting the talent strategy, Washington followed a passive approach to recruitment—post an opening, process applications. Now, Washington recruiters aggressively poach talent from pools outside of the city, including the fabled Montgomery County, Maryland, and Fairfax County, Virginia, school systems. In this, Rhee hoped to reverse a long established brain drain of excellent African American teachers to those suburban school districts. Talent managers in Washington scan school districts in nearby states to identify schools that have seen sharp increases in performance and send these principals a letter of congratulations—and a pitch to work in Washington. They follow up with a phone call and encourage the principals to visit. For principals who work far away, Washington arranges "webinars" led by top leaders to answer questions about the city. Candidates are tracked, and the chancellor monitors the process monthly. This aggressive approach is part of shifting the central office culture—not just its organizational chart—so that it stresses commitment, engagement, and accountability.

The less nationally prominent cities in our study also sought to retain and reward the best teachers and principals, but generally they have not sought new talent or transformed their human resource practices as aggressively as the school districts described above. Other cities such as Hartford, in a somewhat less talent-rich area, recruit nationally but have not become the kind of magnet for talent that similar-sized districts, like New Orleans and Washington, have become due to restrictive state certification rules. One response to that has been an important collaboration between Hartford and Achievement First, a high-performing charter school network. Achievement First has been training small cohorts of school leaders identified by Hartford Public Schools to be the next generation of Hartford school leaders.

In the current recession, all school districts have been forced to limit their hiring, but some continue to use every opportunity to attract exceptionally talented people and make them available to struggling schools. Given the current high rate of unemployment, teachers and administrators are staying in their jobs. But if the recession lingers, the recruitment of new talent, so essential to the success of portfolio strategies, will be difficult to sustain.

Sources of Support for Schools

The traditional district model of public education is based on schools that are opened and managed by a central office and on services to support those schools, also provided by a central office. The problems with this model are that schools get only what the school district has to offer: sometimes districts invest in services that schools don't need, and schools often come to regard the assistance as just another central office regulation. Additionally, the model is not disciplined to be efficient; school support controls a large part of the district budget but is not subject to competition or productivity pressures.

Portfolio leaders realize that being the sole provider of services to schools is expensive and often ineffective. Principals complain about the quality and availability of services, claiming that they have to take what the central office is equipped to give them. Giving principals control over their budgets means they could purchase the services they find most useful. These leaders also realize that the central office is just one source of talent and ideas, and that in fact charter schools have developed some very successful models that could better serve some students.

External Providers. Efforts to encourage greater school-based initiative and variety often run up against the rigid structure of central offices. Central office units intended to help improve instruction often have some expertise and not others; schools that need something for which the central office is not staffed could be out of luck. Central offices often regulate schools in ways that go beyond what the school board or superintendent intend.

Portfolio leaders hope to limit such central office control, in part by reducing its staff and capacities but also by creating more diverse assistance organizations to which schools could turn. School per-pupil funding would increase, as central office units are downsized or closed. Schools would then have the money to buy the support services they need, ranging from school-specific professional development, accounting, budgeting, and HR (again, specifically looking out for the needs of individual schools).

In New York and Chicago the number of options available to school leaders is enormous, ranging from professional development providers, set up by colleges and former leaders of central offices, to major multiservice operators like New York's New Visions for Public Schools, which can provide teacher training, board development, leadership training, self-assessment tools, and overall management of entire schools.

The New Orleans RSD leadership did not want to build a large permanent central office. Superintendent Paul Vallas, hoping to rely on independent providers, could find only a few locally. New Schools for New Orleans (NSNO), an independent nonprofit, took on the job of creating an infrastructure of school support organizations. It hoped to encourage new and existing organizations to offer services that autonomous schools need, everything from facilities maintenance and accounting to teacher training and advice on school improvement. NSNO would seed development of these organizations, which would then cover their operating costs from school fees.

The RSD also addressed the problem of services to schools by recruiting charter management organizations (CMOs), which could provide comprehensive services to the schools affiliated with them. The RSD started with the Knowledge Is Power Program (KIPP), whose schools are popular and considered among the highest performing in New Orleans. A senior district staff member also created a new CMO to redevelop formerly direct-run schools. New Orleans is also encouraging the formation of additional local CMOs and trying to attract national school providers. Given the draw on funds from the post-Katrina population decline and charter school proliferation, the school district believes that, in order to be financially sustainable, it must shave off support operations and become a broker of the services needed by schools rather than a central provider.

Denver has relied on its thriving nonprofit sector to offer similar forms of assistance to autonomous schools and to take on planning projects (such as the integrated choice and enrollment system). Leaders of Denver's new schools office have also recruited CMOs that, like those in New Orleans, can provide services to their schools, thus reducing the need for a large central office. However, in Denver, Chicago, Hartford, and Baltimore, large numbers of district-run schools still depend on the central office and are limited by its capacity. If these school districts are to implement the portfolio strategy fully, they will need to do more to change these schools' freedom of action, control of funds, and freedom to purchase services. Tennessee's new Achievement School District (which is taking over chronically low-performing schools from across the state) is working on building these services. The district has been connecting with charter management organizations to build a bank of service providers for everything from speech therapy to custodial services.

In addition to building new capacities and greater flexibility of provision, reliance on independent support organizations also creates new sources of support for and commitment to the portfolio-based strategy. It also serves the purpose of moving the district away from providing the services and into the role of regulator, allowing schools to choose the support they find most useful under pressure for results.

New School Providers. When districts decide to provide options for children in unproductive schools, they must identify groups of educators capable of running schools that will be coherent and effective. Some of these groups might be found inside the district (for example, groups of principals and teachers who have an idea how they would work together if given the freedom to put their plans into action). However, in big cities with large university-educated populations and many colleges and non-profit groups with educational expertise, internal groups are not the only possible new school providers. To offer many new options, and to make sure children get the best possible new schools, leaders of portfolio districts look both inside and outside their districts.

In New Orleans, with no existing schools, the RSD relied entirely on outside groups, both local and national. State Superintendent Cecil Picard and his successor, Paul Pastorek, expected to charter all the new schools. However, the return rate of students in the 2006–07 school year was so fast that the RSD could not find enough qualified charter operators to meet the demand. Groups prepared to run good charter high schools were in particularly short supply. The RSD therefore created a limited number of "direct-run" schools—in effect, schools run by individuals who could not have won a charter. Because direct-run schools have not produced student gains nearly as decisively as the charter schools, the RSD is once again trying to assign all schools to independent providers. The RSD is encouraging formation of small CMOs led by successful local school leaders to take over and redevelop the direct-run schools.

New York has given new freedom to groups of school employees and has relied on nonprofit groups with relevant expertise. A good example is New Visions for Public Schools, a nonprofit organized to create new schools in low-income areas of New York City twenty years before Chancellor Klein and Mayor Bloomberg came onto the scene. These New York and New Orleans programs, in addition to Chicago's Renaissance 2010 initiative, were built on existing nonprofits, encouraged formation of others, and recruited national school suppliers like KIPP, Achievement First, and Green Dot.

In seeking to open a hundred new schools during its Renaissance 2010 initiative, Chicago sought to attract some well-known national providers. But the initiative mainly relied on established local organizations recruited and sponsored by an independent, business-funded philanthropy, the Renaissance Schools Fund. Chicago also created several categories of "earned autonomy" schools—high-performing, district-run schools judged to be able to make good use of control over budgets, hiring, instructional materials, and daily schedules. In 2011, with the arrival of new superintendent Jean-Claude Brizard, Chicago also began recruiting nationally to increase its rate of new school formation.

Denver, Baltimore, and Hartford also sought to encourage new local school providers and attract established national groups. Their moderate but steady rates of new school formation have required philanthropic investment and creation of new schools' offices in the district headquarters. In the case of Denver, they also pursued a "grow your own" strategy by replicating the highly successful West Denver Prep charter school five more times (these schools are now called Strive Preparatory Schools). These districts have also not encountered the kinds of supply problems (more new schools needed than providers available for them) that have sometimes plagued New Orleans and also New York and Chicago.

Performance-Based Accountability

With autonomy comes accountability. In a portfolio district, accountability involves much more than simply publishing school scores or swapping school leaders, which is typical in districts where schools' existence is not contingent on performance. Portfolio district leaders accept responsibility for ensuring that every child has a good school and that the district has the tools to accomplish this, tools that leaders in conventional districts lack. Accountability in a portfolio district involves natural consequences. Effective teachers and schools get strong support; when failures occur, district leaders must find a better way to educate the children placed at risk.[16]

School teams can approach learning from any angle. What matters is that they get results and operate an organization that teachers want to teach in and that students and families want to be in. Portfolio districts have developed school report cards that illustrate how each school is doing. These are very complicated beneath the surface and are not without flaws, but they provide multiple measures of school performance for every school in the district and are made public on the district website.

In most traditional districts, school closures are usually the result of shrinking budgets and declining enrollment. Portfolio districts take the bold and often unpopular step of closing schools based on performance. There may be a host of reasons why the school is not succeeding—some of them are even the fault of the district. Regardless of the reason, when children are not thriving in the current arrangement, a new program, and often new leadership and staffing, are needed.

Measuring Performance. Portfolio districts use performance measures to guide school improvement efforts and to decide which schools merit rewards, expansion, renewal, or closure. Measuring school performance is a complex endeavor. District leaders need excellent indicators about school, student, and teacher performance, indicators that provide information about how well the portfolio is functioning. They need measurements of net performance—of a school's value-added, holding all else equal. Districts may rely heavily on standardized testing, while also analyzing tests in light of student and neighborhood characteristics and other indicators of school climate and organizational health. In New York City, schools get an annual letter grade based on student progress, student performance, school environment, and the achievement gap (figure 2-3). New York City's school report cards are greatly anticipated and publicly released every fall.

Most portfolio districts use multiple measures of student performance, including test scores and other measures of progress through school and graduation. At a minimum, performance measurement involves

—Status measures: At what level are students in the school performing?

—Gain measures: How much does the average student in a school gain on a performance indicator (test scores, course completion)?

—Comparison with like students and schools: How does the school compare to other schools serving similar students?

The core of all districts' performance measurements are test scores, normally on a state-mandated test that is administered at least once each year. Portfolio district leaders try hard to make fair comparisons of like against like, though these comparisons are never perfect. Schools serving similar proportions of poor or disadvantaged students can differ in unmeasured ways, and these, not quality of instruction, might cause apparent performance differences. Despite the aim to avoid making inappropriate comparisons, things can go wrong. A small adjustment factor in New York City's school report cards produced extremely different results for the same schools over a two-year period (2008 and 2009).

Many portfolio districts are adopting the Colorado Growth Model, based on Denver's experience (figure 2-4). This model compares every student's annual growth with that of all the other students in the state who scored at the same percentile the year before. The results are more stable and easier to explain than the complex algorithms previously used in New York and elsewhere. It provides an intuitively meaningful display, arraying

FIGURE 2-3. New York City Report Card

NYC Department of Education
Dennis M. Walcott, Chancellor

Progress Report 2010-11

Academy of Hospitality and Tourism		OVERALL GRADE	**B**

PRINCIPAL:	Adam Breier	OVERALL SCORE	**59.4** out of 100
DBN:	17K408		
ENROLLMENT:	310		
SCHOOL TYPE:	High School	PERCENTILE RANK	**40**
PEER INDEX:	1.97		

(see p. 7 for more details on peer index)

This school's overall score is greater than or equal to that of 40 percent of High Schools.

Overall Grades - High School

GRADE	SCORE RANGE	% OF SCHOOLS
A	70.0 or higher	33% of schools
B	58.0 - 69.9	32% of schools
C	47.0 - 57.9	24% of schools
D	40.0 - 46.9	8% of schools
F	39.9 or lower	4% of schools

For high schools, grades are based on cut scores determined prior to the release of the Progress Report. Further, schools with a four year graduation rate in the top third citywide cannot receive a grade lower than a C. Schools in their first year, without a graduating class or in phase out receive a report with no grade or score.

Overview

Each school's Progress Report (1) measures student year-to-year progress, (2) compares the school to peer schools and (3) rewards success in moving all children forward, especially children with the greatest needs. Strong Progress Report results are the basis for monetary rewards for school leaders, and poor results are an important factor in determining whether schools require intensive support or intervention. For more information, see schools.nyc.gov/community/planning/Support+and+Intervention.htm.

CATEGORY	SCORE		GRADE	DESCRIPTION
Student Progress	31.2 out of 60		C	Student Progress measures the annual progress students make toward meeting the state's graduation requirements by earning course credits and passing state Regents exams.
Student Performance	16.4 out of 25		B	Student Performance measures how many students graduated within 4 and 6 years of starting high school, and the types of diplomas they earned.
School Environment	8.8 out of 15		B	School Environment measures student attendance and a survey of the school community rating academic expectations, safety and respect, communication, and engagement.
Closing the Achievement Gap	3.0 (14 max)			Schools receive additional credit for exceptional graduation and/or Regents outcomes by students with disabilities, English Language Learners, and students who enter high school at the lowest performance level.
Overall Score	59.4 out of 100		B	The overall grade is based on the total of all scores above, including additional credit for closing the achievement gap. Category scores may not add up to total score because of rounding.

Performance over time

Percentile rank of this school's overall Progress Report score for the past three years:

The Progress Report is a one-year snapshot of a school's performance. The Progress Report methodology has evolved over time, in response to school and community feedback, changes in state policy, and higher standards. For a description of methodology changes, visit schools.nyc.gov/ProgressReport.

Other accountability measures

These measures are separate from the Progress Report, and are an important part of school accountability in New York City and State.

Quality Review	State Accountability
The school's most recent Quality Review Score:	The school's current status:
Developing	**In Good Standing**
2010-11	2010-11

The Quality Review is an observational evaluation conducted by an experienced educator, focused on how well a school is organized to educate its students.

This status is determined by the New York State Department of Education under the No Child Left Behind Act.

---

every school in the city (charters included) on a figure with four quadrants: High rate of gain, high status (absolute scores); low rate of gain, high status; high rate of gain, low status; and low rate of gain, low status. It is easy to see what schools are improving, holding their own, stagnant but at a fairly high level, or falling further behind.

FIGURE 2-4. **Student Performance, by Growth Versus Income Status, Denver Middle Schools, 2011[a]**

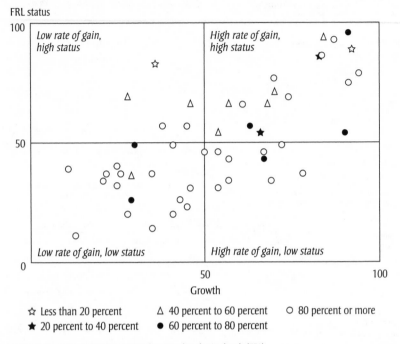

FRL status

Low rate of gain, high status

High rate of gain, high status

Low rate of gain, low status

High rate of gain, low status

Growth

☆ Less than 20 percent   △ 40 percent to 60 percent   ○ 80 percent or more
★ 20 percent to 40 percent   ● 60 percent to 80 percent

a. Percentages indicate students getting free or reduced-price lunch (FRL).

The Colorado Growth Model codes schools by their proportion of students eligible for free or reduced-price lunches (a measure of poverty). Figure 2-4 shows that several schools serving low-income students are also high on both growth and status measures. It also shows some schools with higher income students not making growth or achievement. Users of the district's website can place a cursor over a particular dot on the chart and get the name of the school represented. Parents can get similarly detailed information on their child and his or her school. Children's growth rates are based on comparisons with other children in Colorado who started at the same percentile level on the state's achievement test.

These measures are the start, not the end, of the accountability process. New York and Denver look closely at the circumstances of all the schools in the low-low quadrant, asking whether new leadership or student population changes might explain or exacerbate the school's problems. No district uses these data alone to decide what is to be done about a school.

Managing the School Portfolio. New York, Denver, Chicago, Hartford, Boston, and New Orleans have created new portfolio management offices, whose job it is to look beneath the hard data and decide what is to be done about a struggling school. These offices consider many factors other than performance:

—Demographic trends affecting the numbers, ages, and characteristics of students in different neighborhoods

—Family choice data, including preference patterns of families in different neighborhoods and lists of schools with long waiting lists and schools that few parents choose

—Location, condition, capacity, and vacancy of school facilities by neighborhood

—Plans and schedules for new school construction, renovation, or abandonment by neighborhood

—Availability of lease properties suitable for school use by neighborhood

—Transportation options to all existing and prospective school locations

—Walking routes to all existing and prospective school locations

—Availability of qualified school leaders and lead teachers in current recruitment and training pipelines

—Characteristics, capacities, and track records of charter operators and other providers who could assume responsibility for a new or phased-in school

Taken together, these factors can suggest what might be done for the children in the existing school, including trying to improve the school as it stands, giving children chances to transfer to better schools nearby, or replacing the school with a charter school with a specific mission suitable to the neighborhood.

Closing Schools. Though it can be tempting to simply close a school whose students do not perform and let the students find their way to better schools, portfolio districts have a responsibility to ensure that students whose school is closed truly will be better off. Unfortunately, some school closing decisions, particularly in the early phases of Chicago's Renaissance 2010, might not have considered all the consequences, forcing children into equally bad options and unsafe conditions farther from home. Even school closings in localities that proceeded more carefully often were not accepted by parents and the public. New York City's early closings, which focused on schools widely considered to be dangerous and disgraceful, were far less controversial than later closings that affected low-performing schools that were serving their custodial purposes adequately.

When schools close, teachers and administrators lose jobs, students experience disrupted routines, cherished sports teams are disbanded, and friendships are broken. Affected groups have strong incentives to protest the closure. In some districts, these protests may become especially charged when they involve racial politics. Conflict can arise even in places where coalitions may form to support the closure of low-performing schools. School closures in a portfolio district require transparency and communication. They require significant efforts to address and manage tensions and conflict so that they do not derail the reform and, where possible, they marshal support for the reform.[17]

Districts that have experienced little friction during school closures have good ways of showing families what they could have. For example, Hartford's long history with attractive and oversubscribed magnet schools paved the way for underserved communities to want something similar in place of low-performing schools. Successful districts have also developed clear criteria for closure so that there is no mystery surrounding the decision. In Oakland, schools are funded based on enrollment. If enrollment declines for several years, funding declines, and principals make the call over whether to try to attract more families or phase out the school. New schools created in place of a closed school can keep the name, if it's a source of community pride.

Districts also can keep the children in place and bring in new operators. If children do need to move, districts must ensure that families know exactly where the children will go and that it's obviously a better place. Despite the upset and noise surrounding school closure and reopening decisions, many cities report that the noise abruptly stops on the day the new school opens and the children meet their teachers.

No closure, replacement, phase out, phase in, or any other kind of turnaround is without upset. Even districts that have tried to learn from mistakes are still a long way from solving the problem of a low-performing school with a constituency—which is every low-performing school.

Public Engagement

Like most bold initiatives in the public sector, the portfolio strategy requires widespread support—which does not come automatically. Many citizens have tuned out from public education or simply learned to expect the worst. Several elements of the portfolio strategy are sure to create conflict. Placing charter schools in the same buildings as traditional public schools, basing teacher evaluations in part on student achievement, closing down low-performing schools—these scenarios all have the potential to sort stakeholders into opposing camps, both of which feel like they are losing out. (Chapters 4 and 6 explore in detail the conflicts associated with portfolio strategies and how city leaders try to manage them.)

Portfolio district leaders often underestimate the political challenges they face. If communications aren't handled well, though, and change mobilizes enough opposition, it doesn't matter how well leaders analyze data and target action, they may still be denied the chance to continue on their path toward progress.

The wrenching and relentless changes that have taken place in New York City over a decade have left many New Yorkers feeling as though things are worse off than before Bloomberg took office, even though much of the evidence is to the contrary. Nine years into the work, almost 75 percent of public school parents feel that things are about the same or worse.[18] And yet graduation rates and achievement rates for all students steadily—and, for some groups, dramatically—increased.

Few districts have figured out how to make progress while attending closely to process—portfolio districts are known for developing bold plans and launching them, all the while hoping the that "doing the right thing" on behalf of children and the hoped-for outcomes will be enough to convince people that it was a good idea. This, of course, is not how the public sector works. Officials get some points for caring and being decent, but these count for little when controversy arises. New initiatives, even those that eventually make important progress, seldom work so dramatically that results are immediately evident. However, portfolio district leaders, in general, have neglected public engagement, failing to build a communications strategy or to gather data that might prove their case.

In Washington, former chancellor Michelle Rhee refused the offer of a free full-time communications adviser and then proceeded to alienate many constituencies. She did develop important support among the business elite; it was not enough to save her job but was enough to get a successor appointed who would carry on with the same strategy. Some portfolio district leaders have worked much harder at public engagement than did Michelle Rhee. Joel Klein, for example, put in countless hours in churches and community meetings, but parents and educators still considered him remote and unresponsive. In contrast, RSD leaders in New Orleans shunned public meetings for a long time while they worked desperately to get new schools started. Many New Orleanians credit Paul Vallas and Paul Pastorek for fast action but still condemn them for failing to consult. This judgment might not be fair, but based on the experience of all the portfolio districts, it is inevitable. Former superintendents Steven Adamowski in Hartford and Arne Duncan in Chicago also put in their time in public forums but were still condemned for "shooting first and asking questions later."

In Denver, where support for the portfolio strategy constantly hangs on a one-vote margin on the school board, superintendents Michael Bennet and then Tom Boasberg have both been strategic about public engagement and generated new sources of support. They learned the value of working quietly with key groups before rolling out big initiatives. At the same time, however, opponents continue refining the case against them. In the case of Denver's school closure efforts, portfolio leaders have learned a lot about public engagement and the limitations of even their best efforts.[19] Only one portfolio district leader, Andres Alonso of Baltimore, has enjoyed consistently high public support; this, ironically, stems more from an engaging personality and an ability to inspire confidence than from a full explanation of and consultation about the actions about to be taken.

There may be no way to prevent conflict, but most districts have left a great deal of room to be more attentive to communicating their goals and plans and seeking feedback. Some districts allocate funds to marketing, but districts actually need to hire a professional public relations firm, just like every other major business and political campaign. They need the benefit of an outside third party who can translate the district's work to the public and gauge the public's reaction. District leaders can't afford to neglect public engagement. They need to do a better job of conveying what they are trying to do, why people should support it, and what families and communities can expect to gain. Again and again, the public needs to be convinced of how the changes will help their children and where they have already done so.

Conclusion

The number of districts pursuing the portfolio strategy in 2012 is approaching thirty. They share many similarities, but as is evidenced in this chapter, districts differ in where they start and how quickly they implement the strategy. All, however, are learning that they can't get the benefits of the strategy without implementing all seven components of the portfolio strategy (box 2-1).

The next chapter examines more deeply how cities come to adopt the portfolio strategy.

CHAPTER THREE

How the Portfolio Strategy Gets Adopted: A Tale of Two Cities

Though their house was in Denver, Marco's parents sent his older brother and sister to schools in a neighboring district, taking advantage of the interdistrict choice program in Colorado. His parents thought the suburban school was safer and more caring than the school in their neighborhood. But as they got ready to send Marco to school for the first time in 2009, they heard about the new schools that the Denver district was opening nearby. They also saw a TV program about the Denver superintendent, who said that the city was offering new choices and hoped parents would consider keeping their children in the city.

The suburban school that Marco's sister attended reached out to the family, hoping he would enroll there too. They also saw fliers about new Denver charter schools and were invited to an open house with the new principal and teachers. A disgruntled neighbor said the unaccustomed attention to where children go to school was all about the money. Marco's father agreed, but he saw nothing wrong with it. Why shouldn't schools compete to enroll Marco, just as private schools did for kids who could pay tuition?

Marco's mother and father chose a new charter school, which they liked more and more as Marco passed from kindergarten into first grade. They also paid a lot more attention to news coverage of the Denver school superintendent, who seemed to approach his job in the manner of a chief executive officer of a business enterprise. Marco's mother was surprised at how direct and unsentimental he was when he talked about schools and achievement, but she thought he made sense.

What Leads a City to Adopt a Portfolio Strategy?

Cities that adopt portfolio strategies have some things in common: most have widely recognized problems of school effectiveness, especially for low-income and minority children, and have long histories of seeking improvement. Many have financial problems, caused either by declining enrollment, an aging and therefore more expensive teacher force, un-funded retiree pension and benefits costs, a mismatch between the location of school buildings and current residential patterns, and long-deferred building maintenance.

Mayoral takeover of the schools, as exemplified by Adrian Fenty in Washington and Michael Bloomberg in New York City, is widely recognized as the foundation of some portfolio strategies. However, portfolio strategies have also been introduced by aggressive school superintendents with the support of school board majorities (Denver, Rochester, Hartford, and Baltimore), with and without mayoral support (with such support in Los Angeles, Denver, Cleveland, and Hartford, without such support in Baltimore), by state officials assigned to oversee city schools in crisis (New Orleans and Oakland), and by a school board responding to grassroots pressure (Los Angeles). What all these cities have in common is a political change that weakens support for an existing system and transfers authority to persons and groups who want to follow an un-precedented line of action.

Cities pursuing portfolio strategies are neither like happy families—all alike—nor like unhappy families—all different. All portfolio districts are in states that have charter school laws and that are not prevented from creating new charter schools by a legislative cap. All have experimented in the past with creation of new schools, often via a magnet initiative. All have a history of allowing some family choice among public schools. Table 3-1 summarizes other precursor circumstances in each of the eight cities we studied.

—In all cases but Cleveland, portfolio strategies are adopted soon after a new superintendent (or chancellor or CEO) takes office, not in the mid-dle of a superintendent's term. These new leaders are often outsiders, recruited from outside the city, or locals drawn from professions other than education. Increasingly, leaders hired to start or continue portfolio strategies are found in New York City, from among Klein's former close

TABLE 3-1. **Precursors to Adoption of Portfolio Strategies, Eight Cities**

City	New outsider leaders	Political change	Special state law	Union receptivity
New York	Joel Klein, antitrust lawyer	Mayoral takeover	Eliminates school board	Teacher salary increases
New Orleans	Paul Pastorek, lawyer; Paul Vallas, city administrator; John White, TFA and NTC schools administrator	Hurricane	RSD authority; employment termination	Void all contracts
Washington	Michelle Rhee, policy advocate	Mayoral takeover	Eliminates school board	Two-tiered contract
Chicago	Arne Duncan, activist	Mayoral takeover	Lifts charter cap	Union infighting, bad PR
Denver	Michael Bennet and Tom Boasberg, both lawyers and bankers	Incremental, with mayor's support	Charter law, innovative schools act	ProComp agreement, leadership
Hartford	Steven Adamowski, radical superintendent	Increased mayoral influence	Mayor appoints board members	Superintendent and union in battle over LIFO
Baltimore	Andres Alonso, from NYC leadership	Power shifts, local board to mayor or governor	Governor and mayor share board appointment	Charter schools required to abide by district union contract
Cleveland	None initially; key central office leaders from other portfolio districts	Dominant mayor's strategy change, alliance with governor	Extensive new enabling legislation	Union excluded from initial coalition, invited in once basic strategy established

collaborators (Andres Alonso in Baltimore, Jean-Claude Brizard in Chicago, and John White in New Orleans), or from among former superintendents working in foundations and think tanks (Steven Adamowski in Hartford).

—Changes that upset the normal politics of the city, whether a mayoral takeover, a sudden change in the mayor's policies (as documented below for Cleveland), a natural disaster, a financial emergency, or widespread skepticism about the school district's competence, precede adoption of a portfolio strategy.[1]

—Cities adopting portfolio strategies almost always receive special attention in state law either in the form of emergency mayoral or state takeover or special powers granted to the superintendent or school board (for example, Colorado's new innovative schools law).

—Portfolio strategies often emerge at times when unions are unusually receptive, either because of unconventional leadership or because they are weakened by bad public relations or internal conflicts.

We cannot say for sure, however, whether these patterns of events make a portfolio strategy inevitable or how quickly a city will adopt one. For many years, Detroit, Dayton, St. Louis, and Kansas City have all had many of the attributes identified in table 3-1, yet to date only Detroit has adopted a portfolio strategy, and that after many years of trying other things. Nor is it always obvious when movement toward the portfolio strategy began in a city. Even in New Orleans, where the hurricane changed everything, there was a pre-Katrina coalition in favor of attracting new school providers to the city and a state law allowing formation of a recovery school district. As Charles Kerchner and colleagues show, in Los Angeles elements that ultimately came together into a portfolio strategy can be seen years and even decades before anyone consciously adopted the full strategy.[2]

However, as Cleveland's recent all-out adoption of the portfolio strategy shows, nothing explains the adoption of this strategy as well as the simple decision by a leader or a local coalition to do so. Though the portfolio strategy is increasingly common in big cities, it represents a sharp departure from long-established ways of doing business. Changes of this magnitude don't come about easily. They arise from a sense of crisis: Important people in a city must come to believe that the existing arrangements for providing schools simply will not meet the city's needs for an educated population and workforce. Then some person or group must step forward to challenge the existing arrangement, formulate an alternative to it, and gain the political authority to act.

With the exception of New Orleans, where after Hurricane Katrina it was difficult to see what other approach would be possible, the cities adopting the portfolio strategy were not always the ones with the worst school systems or the least grassroots support for the existing school system.[3] They were among the large number of cities where large numbers of poor and minority students have less than a fifty-fifty chance of graduating from high school, and where an identifiable set of schools always reports the lowest test scores, highest student absenteeism, and highest teacher turnover. But for every city that has adopted the portfolio strategy there is another—a Dayton, St. Louis, Pittsburgh, Miami—that has not done so.

> *Nothing explains the adoption of a portfolio strategy as well as the simple decision by a leader or local coalition to do so.*

Adoption of the portfolio strategy comes about in localities where there is both widespread concern about the performance of the school district and people who have particular ideas and the determination to act on them. Most of the initiators of the strategy knew something about the idea and knew others who were thinking about it. City leaders we interviewed in New Orleans, Hartford, New York, and Denver said they knew our earlier publications about the portfolio strategy, including *It Takes a City* and articles about post-Katrina options for New Orleans.[4] Recently, the people who led portfolio strategy adoptions in Baltimore, Rochester, Newark, New Orleans, and New Haven had worked closely with Joel Klein in New York City. Paul Vallas carried some ideas from Chicago to Philadelphia and thence to New Orleans.

Once the idea of the portfolio strategy is raised in a city and gains significant political support, it must still be transformed from abstract principles into a set of reform initiatives. This chapter discusses how this happened, and how in two cities with very different politics (Denver and New York) resistance and other local factors channeled the strategy's development. We focus on these cities because they represent different ends of the spectrum of political change, with New York's coming via a revolutionary mayoral appointment, which eliminated most forums for political opposition, and Denver's coming over time and incrementally as a result of steady superintendent leadership in a system where the school board, union, and other competing centers of power remained intact.

Portfolio Strategy, New York City

A year after Michael Bloomberg was elected mayor of New York in 2001, he gained control of the city's troubled $22 billion school district. At the time, the city's 1 million students were struggling, with roughly only 35 percent of eighth-grade students passing the New York State English Language Arts Test and only 27 percent of them passing the math test. The city's four-year graduation rate hovered at 48 percent.

In approving Bloomberg's takeover of the schools, the state legislature disbanded the school board and put the mayor fully in charge. In May 2002 he appointed Joel Klein, an antitrust lawyer and communications company executive, as chancellor. Bloomberg did not have any particular ideas about a portfolio strategy, but Klein did. With some fits and starts (and some learning and changes of direction along the way), Klein aggressively built the portfolio strategy for more than eight years before resigning as chancellor in late 2010.

One close associate of Klein's explains the premises on which Klein, his associates, and the mayor agreed: "The [pre-2002] school system does what it was built to do: make stable jobs, accommodate the demands of interest groups and comply with state laws. It can do those things without providing effective schools for all kids. We intended to rebuild the system around a new mission, one that puts children and their learning first." In general, Bloomberg operated as a CEO of a conglomerate, overseeing a trusted and competent CEO of one of the conglomerate's businesses. He did not dictate Klein's actions, but he did want to be consulted and informed, not surprised.

Klein's approach to systemwide reform was not clear, at least to observers, in his first few years. Though the mayoral takeover had given him tremendous freedom of action, he did things that conventional superintendents might have done: hired a high-profile instructional leader, mandated citywide use of a reading method, and took some powers away from local subdistrict superintendents. However, after a year in office, Klein started to strengthen the hand of principals and reengineer the system to become a supporter of strong schools, not a source of mandates about instructional method. He had concluded that there was no one best model for all the schools in the city and that experimentation, not central planning, was the key to rapid improvement, and thus the commitment to the portfolio strategy.

After his first year, Klein reorganized the system several times, incrementally cutting the powers and staffing of the central bureaucracy, expanding school autonomy (via increased school control over staffing and spending decisions and choice of professional development providers), and strengthening his immediate leadership team's ability to hold school leaders accountable for performance.

Enabling Autonomy

The key action in this process was the creation of an autonomy zone, in 2004. That year twenty-nine schools were selected to gain control over key staffing and spending decisions in return for strict accountability for performance. Low-performing schools in the zone could be restaffed or closed and replaced with new schools, including charters. Schools in the autonomy zone were funded on the basis of enrollment, did not have to accept the most senior teacher who applied for a vacancy, and could select their own sources of instructional assistance and teacher professional development. After a one-year trial of the autonomy zone, Klein expanded it very quickly, to sixty schools the second year, 321 the third year, and to most of the schools in the city in 2006–07.

Klein and his leadership team hoped that the new principals' academy, created in 2003, would offer relevant training and assistance. Deputy chancellors under Klein's instructions also created new procedures to identify teachers with obvious leadership skills but no administrator credentials and to recruit them into a series of rotations that would prepare them to become principals.

Expanding school autonomy systemwide required major changes in policy. Robert Gordon, a member of Klein's core leadership team, designed a new school funding system, which allocated most state and local funds directly to schools, based on enrollment (weighted to take account of student risk factors). Few other cities adopting features of New York's reforms are so clear about the uses of autonomy. Hartford and Washington, for example, still treat autonomy as a reward.

In 2005 the city's Department of Education (DOE) and the United Federation of Teachers (UFT) also built a systemwide collective bargaining agreement that allowed a school's principal–in collaboration with the school's teachers–to ignore seniority in all teacher-hiring decisions. This amounted to abandonment of a core tenet of teacher unionism. Union leaders explained the agreement as being in teachers' interest. As one union leader said in an interview, "Any time we can help teachers gain greater control over their working environments, we will do so."

We intended to rebuild the school system around a new mission, one that puts children and their learning first.

The devolution strategy had its complement in the central office. Klein took as much business as possible away from established central office bureaus and had key decisions made by members of his small leadership team. He created new talent, accountability, and portfolio management offices, which subsumed existing human resources and assessment functions, and put members of his immediate leadership team in charge.

Klein's Leadership Team

Klein created a small coherent leadership team, initially composed of approximately fifteen New Yorkers with broad experience in business, law, education, government, and nonprofits. Many of them shared Klein's antitrust views. When Klein took office, the vast New York City schools bureaucracy looked a lot like a business monopoly, and the leadership team wanted to break its grip and set off competition and innovation.

Starting in Klein's first year and increasingly thereafter, the leadership team took charge of key parts of the system, including design of a new data-based school accountability system, the general counsel's office, funds distribution and financial oversight, talent (teacher and principal recruitment, development, and assignment), in-service teacher and principal training, portfolio management (monitoring the overall supply of schools to identify high performers, unmet needs, and schools in trouble), and overall operations management.

The leadership group has also included career educators, such as lawyer-educator Andres Alonso and the widely admired school principal Eric Nadelstern, who served as communication links between Klein and rank-and-file educators. Nadelstern, Alonso, and others (such as the current senior deputy chancellor and chief academic officer, Shael Polikoff Suransky) have been trusted both to constrain Klein's initiatives, so they would be tolerable to educators, and to make the case for the reforms to rank-and-file educators. The senior counselor, Michele Cahill, who had developed strategies for small high schools nationwide for the Carnegie Corporation of New York, was perhaps the chief "boundary spanner" on the leadership team, until mid-2007, when she left to rejoin the Carnegie Corporation.

Membership in Klein's leadership team changed over time, as individuals left to return to their core professions or went elsewhere to lead reform strategies. (Alonso is now CEO of the Baltimore Public Schools.) Assignments with the core leadership also shifted every year or so. Leadership team members say this was meant to ensure that team members did not become highly specialized or captured by the part of the system they oversee. By 2009 the number of educators on the team increased, so that educators were doing jobs previously assigned only to people with roots in law and business. The educators brought into the leadership team were generally drawn from teachers and principals who had worked on earlier Klein initiatives, such as small schools and the autonomy zone.

Sustaining School Autonomy

Mayoral control and the absence of a school board can mean that the chancellor has a constituency of one. However, that does not exempt the chancellor and his leadership team from paying attention to politics. School system leaders can lose the mayor's confidence and even contribute to the mayor's downfall, if they cause unnecessary firestorms (as was demonstrated in the defeat of Washington's mayor, Adrian Fenty, and the subsequent ouster of the school chancellor, Michelle Rhee, in September 2010). Moreover, leaders like Klein, who hope to set the school system permanently on a more productive path, need to build lasting support for what they have done. Klein and his close associates developed a three-part political strategy:

—Build new constituencies in favor of a permanent strategy of devolution to strong, accountable schools.

—Convert groups that traditionally support a centralized, bureaucratic school system.

—Accept that some groups will not support the new model and limit their influence.

The most important element of this political strategy is the first. DOE leaders hoped to activate some groups that had previously paid little attention to public education and to create new organizations whose interests were closely tied to the reform. Groups which Klein hoped to activate included business and media organizations concerned about the quality of the city's workforce; leaders of higher education institutions, such as Hunter College, that trained teachers and leaders for new roles created by the reform; families that might be drawn back to the city's schools from private and suburban schools; and philanthropic foundations. New organizations included the nonprofit organizations that schools can hire to provide assistance with curriculum, assessment, and training; teachers and school leaders whose career opportunities the reform created; and families that felt previously trapped in and poorly served by the public schools. Klein also reached out to the pastors and congregations of African American churches, hoping to convince them that the most disadvantaged children would benefit from the reform. He frequently claimed to hold the world record for time spent in black Christian churches by a Jew.

Avoiding the politics of paralysis: act fast and avoid consultations that could only delay action or dilute results.

Groups to be converted from support for a more traditional system included incumbent and new public school teachers and administrators (including union members), former central office employees who would now get the opportunity to work more effectively in new nonprofit assistance organizations, and parents and members of the public who had come to accept the old system but might change their minds if the reform made schools much fairer and more effective. DOE leaders did not automatically relegate anyone to the status of intransigent opposition. Because they were able to win agreement from the UFT to allow schools to discount seniority preference in hiring, they knew that the most important union would cooperate to some degree. However, they assumed the unions would be hard to move on many other issues.

Leaders also knew that families already highly satisfied with their schools might oppose the reforms, especially pupil-based funding, which reallocated money away from schools that traditionally captured disproportionate public funding—usually those in the most stable and highest income neighborhoods. But Klein and his team hoped those families would be mollified by better overall school performance and better outcomes for disadvantaged students.

At its core, the political strategy depended on key groups' seeing that the reform was both consistent with their interests and good for the city as a whole. That meant the reform had to be put in place quickly and thoroughly so its benefits would be evident. Thus Klein's political strategy required that the DOE avoid the "politics of paralysis" by acting fast and avoiding consultations that could only delay action or dilute results. He and his team believed that this was the only way to attract new supporters and convert parties that care about results above all else. But the strategy also generated opposition, much of it from groups that took the position, "We want better schools, just not this way." School closings, a complement to Klein's strategy of continuously searching for better school providers and better matches to the needs of groups of children, are always rallying points for opposition. In New York as elsewhere, the strength of the opposition has little to do with the performance of the school chosen for closure or the quality of alternatives available. Opponents focus on jobs, neighborhood identity, and general suspicion of "downtown" authority.

By 2009, 60 percent of eighth graders were passing English. Even more—75 percent—were passing math, a gain of forty-eight points.[5] After many years of stagnation, four-year graduation rates increased by twelve points, to 60 percent.

Portfolio Strategy, Denver

Across the country, several years after New York City launched its reforms, Denver began implementing a similar strategy. A study released in April 2007 by the *Rocky Mountain News* and the Piton Foundation found that tens of thousands of the city's children were choosing to attend schools outside the district, leaving the district with half-empty buildings and low-income families with few quality choices.[6] In response, Denver's Board of Education and Superintendent Michael Bennet made a dramatic call for systemic change. "It is hard to admit," they wrote, "but it is abundantly clear that we will fail the vast majority of children in Denver if we try to run our schools the same old way."[7] They argued that change would require the district to "no longer function as a one-size-fits-all, centralized, industrial-age enterprise making choices that schools, principals, teachers, and, most important, parents are in a much better position to make for themselves." The district, they wrote, "needs to function more like a partner, building capacity and leadership at the school level and serving as an incubator for innovation."

Six months later, following the work of an independent citizens committee, the Denver Public Schools (DPS) Board of Education unanimously voted to close eight school buildings and create five new schools in existing buildings. The board also resolved to develop new "innovative and high performing schools, especially secondary schools, by conducting a Request for Proposal (RFP) process to solicit new schools for the 2009 school year and beyond."

Michael Bennet, who became superintendent in 2005, was the key figure in Denver's adoption of the portfolio strategy. But others before him laid important groundwork. Earlier superintendents, particularly Jerry Wartgow, had tried to make school funding more transparent and equitable. A maverick teachers union leader, Brad Jupp, encouraged by Wartgow, had led the creation of new performance pay options for teachers, called ProComp.[8] Earlier school boards had flirted with decentralization to allow individual schools to adapt to the specific needs of their neighborhoods. A strong local nonprofit advocate for school reform, A+ Denver, was organized to support Bennet's efforts.

Colorado also allowed within- and across-district public school choice, so that parents could choose among city schools or between city schools and those in nearby suburbs. Schools near Denver's borders with other districts had experienced steady enrollment losses, which were widely understood to reflect badly on the quality of city schools. Three local foundations, Donnell-Kay, Piton, and Daniels, had consistently pressed Denver superintendents and school boards for bolder reform and were willing to pay up-front costs for new initiatives. Bennet could not have moved so quickly without those antecedents.

Creating New Schools

In Denver, however, there was no real tradition of new school creation. Though Colorado had a charter law, the majority of early charter schools were started in suburbs and smaller towns. Before Bennet, Denver's approach to charters had been to avoid them when possible and endure competition from them when unavoidable. The Denver school district was considering using charters to provide new options before Bennet's administration, but the idea had not yet taken off. Though overall enrollment was stable or growing slightly, many city schools had endured years of enrollment decline due to interdistrict choice and the draw of a few charter schools.

Bennet (who had left his job as chief of staff to Denver's mayor, John Hickenlooper, to become the superintendent) looked deeply into the financial health of the district he had taken on and was immediately alarmed. The district was responsible for its own teacher retirement plan, which had significant unfunded liabilities. As Bennet discovered, the plan would be immediately insolvent if the district succeeded in keeping a higher proportion of its best young teachers, something Bennet had hoped to accomplish in order to increase school performance. Though teachers contributed to the retirement plan as soon as they were hired, their contributions were not vested until they had worked in the city for five years. New teachers who quit before five years left their contributions behind, in effect helping pay benefits for retirees.

Bennet feared that serious efforts to improve the teaching force would put the district into a downward financial spiral. His solution had two parts: persuade the state of Colorado to take responsibility for the teacher retirement fund and increase citywide enrollment. The portfolio strategy was all about reversing the flow of families into suburban districts and creating options in low-income neighborhoods, where parents were demanding better schools. Bennet wanted to experiment with new options, both to draw back families who were departing for suburban schools and to seek higher performance in low-income city neighborhoods.

In a school district with an elected board and division in the community about aggressive reform, Bennet acted cautiously. He worked closely with parents in a fast-growing part of town to channel unrest about school quality into a request for closure of low-performing schools and creation of new options via chartering. He also pressed for the full implementation of ProComp, as a way to attract new teachers to Denver, and supported development of a data system that could display, by school, student test score growth rates and other outcome measures.[9] He encouraged use of charter schools to create options in the poorest neighborhoods and those most likely to suffer defections to neighboring districts.

These actions were highly public, but Bennet did not present them as a specific named strategy that could become the focus of opposition. Instead, he tucked the portfolio strategy into a broader set of initiatives to improve the district via better curriculum, teacher training, and performance pay, called the Denver Plan. When Bennet presented this multilayered plan, school board members supported it but deferred to the superintendent to drive it administratively and to explain it to the public.

Bennet's superintendency was by no means a takeover of the school system by the mayor, although a close alliance with the city certainly improved the school district's access to transportation, facilities, and other assets. Hickenlooper's immense popularity also helped put a floor under Bennet's approval ratings at the most difficult times. Bennet may also have benefited from the presence of the state legislature in Denver. A bipartisan coalition of legislators worked with Bennet and experts from the University of Colorado at Denver to draft and enact the Innovation Schools Act.[10] This act opened the way to "zones of innovative performance," greater school autonomy, and experimentation with new forms of instruction. Bennet also had a good working relationships with two governors, Republican Bill Owens and Democrat Bill Ritter, who spoke in favor of his initiatives and supported charter schools and the Innovation Schools Act.

Still, Bennet created his own support coalition of local foundation executives and heads of academic institutions and cultivated the city's two daily newspapers. When the *Rocky Mountain News* closed in 2008, Bennet maintained a largely supportive relationship with the *Denver Post*. He also built freedom of action by attracting funding from national foundations and by working closely with key local foundations to channel their limited resources into creation of new schools and a new schools office.

Like Klein, Bennet brought experts in finance and management to manage the reform strategy. The most important of these was Tom Boasberg, former communications executive and federal communications regulator. Boasberg became deputy superintendent and developed the data system that allowed district leadership to differentiate schools on the basis of average achievement levels and annual student growth rates. Another corporate strategist, David Suppes, became chief strategy officer and later deputy superintendent. Bennet also relied heavily on an insider, Brad Jupp, the former teachers union negotiator who became a close collaborator on school performance assessment, teacher incentive pay, and development of new options.

Rolling with the Political Punches

Despite his caution in rolling out the portfolio strategy, Bennet encountered increased opposition from the teachers union, and for some months in 2007 he watched as local polls showed his approval ratings to be low.[11]

The strategy of closing some failing neighborhood schools and replacing them with new options, typically charter schools, became more controversial, including in school board elections. The closure of Manual High School (later to be reopened in a smaller new format), in particular, created more political heat. Manual, a storied industrial arts high school that had been a route to good jobs and college for generations of low-income Denver youngsters, had fallen on hard times. It was considered Denver's worst and most dangerous school. With a grant from the Gates Foundation, the Denver school board had tried to break Manual into five smaller schools. This happened before Bennet's watch, and he felt he had to start over once again.

However, the success of some of his new schools initiatives reduced the political heat. By the time Bennet accepted appointment to fill an unexpired term in the U.S. Senate in January 2009, he was popular enough with the school board and the public to win appointment for his preferred successor, Tom Boasberg. By the time Boasberg became superintendent, the portfolio strategy had some momentum among district staff, foundations, and parent groups. The growing number of charter school operators and parents also constituted a new support group, and a new foundation-funded website, Education-News Colorado, greatly increased the volume of information available about reform.

Leaders in both cities jolted their systems into action and overcame bureaucratic inertia by emphasizing leadership over governance.

But a coming school board election was a threat. Teachers union leaders, opposed even to the modest rate of school closing and new school creation Bennet had achieved, ran a slate of candidates in the fall 2009 school board elections. The result was the defeat of one Boasberg supporter and the election of three anti-Boasberg activists, leading to a split board, with three pro and three anti votes and one perceived swing member. That swing member, Nate Easley, was supported by the teachers union, and he became president of the board. Over time, it was clear that he was largely supportive of the portfolio strategy, leading to an unsuccessful recall campaign in April 2011. Earlier that year Boasberg had also lost an invaluable collaborator, Brad Jupp, to the U.S. Department of Education.

This political change forced Boasberg to go slowly. He built a very strong new schools office under the leadership of a widely admired principal, who had started new schools and had recruited an experienced school starter from New York City. Boasberg also made it easier for parents to choose among schools and continually backed pro-portfolio staff in conflicts within the central office. However, in his public statements he emphasized the more conventional elements of his reform strategy and downplayed portfolio language. On the district's website, Boasberg, an avowed trustbuster like Klein in New York, obliquely referred to creation of competition and new options but did not go into detail:

> We must acknowledge that our culture historically has not been one consistently defined by high expectations, service, empowerment, and responsibility. This is partly the result of the fact that our district, like school districts across the country, has operated for generations as a monopoly and has suffered from a monopoly's resistance to fundamental change, a lack of urgency, and an inflexibility that often puts the interests of the system and its adults over and above the needs of our students.

Boasberg continued to use student performance data to identify schools in need of transformation or closure. In 2009 eight new schools opened. The number decreased to seven in 2010 and to three in 2011. Like Klein late in his term as chancellor, Boasberg also recruited fewer people from business into district leadership positions than had Bennet and increasingly relied on staff members from within the school system or on educators with new schools experience in other localities.

Unlike New York and New Orleans, where the portfolio strategy was introduced after a profound shock to the system, Denver was introduced to it by normal school district leadership processes, albeit at a time of great discontent and by nontraditional superintendents. Even today, seven years after Bennet took his first steps toward the strategy, the strategy is constantly under attack in Denver and must be managed carefully. As this is written, the new mayor, Michael Hancock, has become an assertive supporter of the portfolio strategy. The three local foundations and parent groups formed with Bennet's assistance continue to provide a base of support for the portfolio strategy. In fall 2001 opponents tried hard to elect a school board majority that would oust Boasberg, but the voters strengthened his hand by electing a pro-reform majority.

Denver's reforms have had a significant impact in the five years since they were initiated. In 2007 there were twenty-one charter schools. Four years later, in 2011, there were thirty-six, with eighteen of them sharing space or housed in DPS facilities. After years of decline, enrollment in Denver Public Schools has increased by more than 8,000 students since 2007, to 81,000. Student achievement is trending up. In 2007, 23 percent of eighth graders were passing math and 38 percent were passing reading. Two years later, in 2009, 30 percent of them were passing math and 43 percent were passing reading.

Similarities and Differences between New York and Denver

Klein and Bennet took over very different districts: New York serves nearly fifteen times as many students as Denver, and the two cities' politics and histories have little in common. In New York, with literally millions of public school parents and more than 100,000 teachers, it is possible to generate a crowd or a flood of letters on almost any issue. In Denver, a big crowd is a sign of a big issue.

However, leaders in both cities faced powerful central school bureaucracies, unionized and tenured teachers, school buildings occupied by incumbent schools, activist parent groups both demanding change and defending the status quo, and well-founded popular skepticism about whether any reform initiative could make a difference. Leaders in both cities had to jolt their systems into action to overcome bureaucratic inertia. They did this by emphasizing leadership over governance. By leadership we mean the use of discretion by officials to cause change in the organizations they head. In contrast, by governance we mean constraints on leadership via established policies and routines, distributed powers, required consultations, and multiple independent approvals of actions. Before Bennet and Klein-Bloomberg took over their cities' schools, governance constraints were paramount. For example,

—The demands of the elected school board and other oversight bodies limited the superintendent's or chancellor's freedom of action and took up a great deal of his time.

—State requirements governed teacher and principal hiring and school staffing.

—Federal and state laws governed the allocation of money to schools and the work assignments of people who were paid from those funds.

—Union contracts determined how teachers were assigned to schools, how teachers got pay increases, and what work teachers could be assigned.

—Other contracts also governed who could lead a school and limited school leaders' roles. Policies giving janitors control of building keys limited principals' and teachers' access to their own school buildings.

Klein and Bennet both started with symbolic actions demonstrating leadership. Klein moved school system headquarters from a notorious bureaucratic fortress at 110 Livingston St. in Brooklyn to the much smaller and more accessible Tweed Courthouse on the City Hall grounds. He then built his own office and that of his close collaborators in a large round room, where no office was walled off and the chancellor's actions were obvious to everyone. Bennet did not transform the superintendent's office space, but he called for a revolution in how teachers were compensated. He also set up a new schools' office whose mission included identifying ways the old central office was undoing freedoms that schools were supposed to have and invoking Bennet's (and later Boasberg's) authority to resolve new schools' conflicts with the traditional central office.

Pursuing the Business Theory of Decentralization

At the highest level of generality, the portfolio strategy practiced in Denver and New York City emphasized the business theory of decentralization:

—Strengthen the top (the superintendent or chancellor and his immediate leadership team) and bottom (individual schools) against the middle (the traditional central office bureaucracy and employee unions).

—Let local units—that is, the schools—make the consequential decisions that affect their productivity.

—Encourage innovation, centralize accountability via common outcome measures, make jobs and the existence of schools contingent on performance, and continually search for better people and providers.

—Seek continuously to improve the options available to customers (families).

In business, top-level leaders do not abdicate responsibility or stop setting goals or allocating resources away from less productive initiatives and toward more promising ones or rewarding performance and punishing failure. However, top-level leaders cede control over methods to the people doing the day-to-day work—to plant managers, sales groups, R&D units, and so on. Units that use their freedom to get good results are rewarded, but those with bad results are liable to being restaffed or replaced. In business decentralization, the offices dedicated to compliance and control shrink or disappear entirely. They are seen as blurring the organization's focus on its goals, buffering compliant nonperformers from scrutiny, discouraging initiative, and standardizing functions that should be subject to experimentation and continuous improvement.

From the time they took office, Bennet, Boasberg, and Klein wanted everyone to understand that future decisions would not be based on tradition, rules, and rights but rather on performance; and that school leaders who once had no discretion were expected to exercise it. To create freedom of action, Klein changed the city's whole system for funding schools, allocating real dollars (instead of assets purchased by others) directly to schools. He also negotiated changes in teachers union contracts to allow school leaders and incumbent teachers to pick the people who would fill staff vacancies as they occurred. Bennet and Boasberg took advantage of existing teacher contract provisions to increase schools' discretion over staffing and incrementally adapted follow-the-pupil funding schemes. Unlike New York, however, Denver was not able to charge school budgets more for highly paid teachers than for lower salaried ones, thus creating a financial advantage for schools with more experienced and expensive teacher forces.

> *School autonomy is a precondition for school improvement, not a reward for high performance.*

Klein and Bennet wanted all schools, including those that were not performing very well, to gain control over staffing, spending, and use of time. They considered school autonomy to be a precondition for school improvement. Universal school autonomy could, they argued, create room for experimentation and let schools build incrementally on successes. It also allowed leaders at the top of the system to identify schools that could not use their freedom of action to improve. Klein and Bennet foresaw a continuous improvement process in which they would expand or duplicate schools that were making gains and prune away those in which students were not learning.

Portfolio district leaders in some other cities we studied (Hartford, Washington, and Chicago) held a contrasting view: that the typical school lacked leadership or staff capacity necessary to build an effective improvement strategy. They therefore granted autonomy only to the very highest performing schools and tried to use central office services to build up school leaders' skills in hopes they would eventually be able to use autonomy.

Klein and Bennet were under no illusion that every school could use its autonomy well. But they also had no confidence that a weak school could be coached or incrementally built up by the district central office. Some marginal schools, they reasoned, might be able to find and purchase effective help from higher education institutions or nonprofit school improvement groups. These would benefit from control over their funds and methods. However, most marginal schools would not improve markedly; their children would be better served by using chartering to create new schools backed by such community resources as cultural and youth service organizations and by national school providers.

Local Politics, National Audience

Politics might ultimately be local, but education reform leaders can benefit from positive national publicity. Both Klein and Bennet were recognized in the national press and widely discussed, though not always favorably, in books and commentary. Positive national notice is not enough to buttress a reform leader against concerted local opposition, but it does gain a leader some benefit of the doubt with opinion leaders and the neutral press.

Klein and Bennet also received steady support from major national philanthropies and local foundations. This support was focused on developing new capacities and piloting new ideas, not on paying for routine operations. The Gates Foundation supported new schools development early in Klein's term and helped fund Denver's development of new schools and new teacher pay schemes. Gates also joined with Broad and Carnegie, in New York, and with local foundations Daniels, Piton, and Donnell-Kay in Denver to pay for data and analytical systems, new central offices to oversee charters, new school providers, and the closing of the lowest performing schools.

New Orleans and Washington also received significant contributions from national foundations—for new schools development in New Orleans and for extra compensation tied to Michelle Rhee's teacher performance pay plan. Local philanthropy was especially important in supporting New

Schools for New Orleans, a nonprofit that incubated new school providers and fostered development of vendors who could provide charter schools with technical assistance and office help. During the era of Renaissance 2010, Chicago received substantial help from Gates and from local philanthropies and business leaders. Locally based national foundations, MacArthur, Spencer, and Joyce, also continued their long-established custom of supporting Chicago schools.

These donations were crucial because they enabled new investments that school district budgets could not have borne. However, they generally did not significantly increase overall local spending. Leanne Stiefel and Amy Ellen Schwartz estimate that for New York City philanthropic donations amounted to 0.5 percent of the city's $24 billion annual K–12 spending, a proportion not much different than reported in Seattle and other cities that are not pursuing significant reforms.[12]

Of the cities we studied, only Hartford and Cleveland diverge from the pattern of prominent support from national media and national philanthropic support. Though both cities' reform strategies are well covered in local media, they have gained only sporadic attention nationally. And though both have won grants from well-endowed local foundations, the levels of support they gain—whether in absolute terms or in proportion of total spending—is less than the other cities.

Portfolio Adoption in Other Cities

Except for New Orleans, which is unique because the existing system was totally destroyed and a law permitted the state education department to take over dozens of schools, initiation of the portfolio strategy in the other cities fits somewhere between New York and Denver. All the cities except New Orleans had established central office bureaucracies, teachers unions, school boards, and groups of parents organized around particular schools. All also had serious performance problems, especially for poor and minority students and geographically identifiable groups of schools where few if any students were graduating from high school prepared for jobs or higher education.

Portfolio strategy adoption in Hartford started with long-term mayor Eddie Perez's gaining the power to appoint a majority of school board members and his hiring of a nationally known superintendent, Steven Adamowski, who was publicly committed to the portfolio idea. The portfolio strategy in Washington also started with the mayor, when the newly elected Adrian Fenty gained control of the public schools and when, with Joel Klein's advice, he hired Michelle Rhee. In the long run, slowly building understanding and consent among concerned citizens might work as well as unfettered use of executive power.

In Cleveland local foundation officers and supporters of new small high schools had worked for several years to lay the groundwork for the portfolio strategy. But a small fringe activity became city policy in January 2012, when Mayor Frank Jackson issued the sweeping new portfolio-based Cleveland Plan.[13] Jackson, a Democrat and centrist in his eighth year as mayor, had always controlled the school system through school board appointments. He surprised most observers by adopting a dramatically more ambitious reform plan than any he had previously endorsed. Jackson also formed an unlikely partnership with the conservative Republican governor of Ohio, John Kasich, to press for legislation to allow much more aggressive creation of new schools and limitations on senior teachers' ability to "bump" teachers in those schools during times of fiscal stress.

> In the long run, slowly building understanding and consent among concerned citizens might work as well as unfettered use of executive power.

Many factors combined to explain Jackson's bold move: serious school district deficits, a determination not to let Cleveland become "another Detroit," widespread resentment of the teachers union's forcing tenured staff members into new schools that had been succeeding with younger, more technically qualified teachers, and growing evidence that children were doing better in the new district-run and charter schools than in traditional public schools. Jackson and local business leaders also saw the bold new plan as the way to build citizen support for new school funding, after many years of unsuccessful levy campaigns. School district CEO Eric Gordon, a traditional educator who had become convinced of the need for the portfolio strategy, and key staff members at the Cleveland and George Gund Foundations, became Mayor Jackson's close allies and implementers.

By contrast, Baltimore adopted the portfolio strategy after ending mayoral control of the schools. The school board hired Klein intimate Andres Alonso from New York City, and he introduced the portfolio idea and carefully built school board support and a broad local coalition. Chicago's portfolio strategy was the most recent of several reforms tried after Mayor Richard Daley gained control of the schools. Arne Duncan crystallized the strategy from parts established by his predecessor, Paul Vallas, but was unable to put it into effect beyond the Southside schools involved in Renaissance 2010. After Duncan's departure, the portfolio strategy went into a limbo in which it was neither abandoned nor actively pursued until the election of Rahm Emanuel in 2011. Emanuel's hand-picked superintendents, first, Jean-Claude Brizard, and later, Barbara Byrd-Bennet, have advanced the portfolio strategy.

Sprint or Marathon?

Comparing these cases, it appears that portfolio adoption can come more suddenly and advance more quickly with mayoral support than when adopted by a board or introduced by a superintendent. However, to out-live the mayor or other major political figure who introduces it, the strategy must ultimately rest on a broader base of support. The slow building of understanding and consent among concerned citizens, which was necessary in cities with functioning school boards such as Baltimore and Denver, might in the long run work as well as the use of executive power—or as in Cleveland, with a combination of both.

Ultimately, Bennet and Boasberg's leadership approach in Denver—going slow; relying on performance data to build support for new schools and school closings; creating elements of the portfolio strategy without publicly tying them together; managing a loose coalition of supporters among foundations, neighborhood groups, and elected officials; and slowly renorming the district's central office via strategic hires—is more likely what is necessary in other cities with functioning school boards (Baltimore, Hartford, Los Angeles) than is the more sudden transformation seen in New York City and New Orleans.

CHAPTER FOUR

Conflict in Portfolio Districts

Judy went all the way through the New York City Public schools and is now the mother of three children attending public schools in Manhattan. She has worked hard to keep standards high in her children's schools, keeping in close touch with teachers and other parents. As she says, "Public school parents don't need to pay tuition, but they pay in other ways. You can't just assume things will be all right."

A confirmed liberal, Judy has always supported efforts to improve schools in poorer parts of the city. But she is very upset about recent developments on New York City schools, especially efforts to force existing schools to share their space with new schools. She says that parents have worked in neighborhood school buildings, improved the library and playground, and fixed up unused classrooms to be used for volunteer work and meetings. Now the city is forcing neighborhood schools to share space with new charter schools that serve kids from other parts of town.

She doesn't like the charter school leaders, some of whom are powerful city politicians, and fears that playgrounds, libraries, and lunchrooms will be crowded and disorderly. She is also angry that the chancellor of the school board and his aides just sprang the so-called colocation plan on parents with only a few months' notice. Judy has talked to the two principals whose schools her children attend, and they are also angry, as are their teachers. Yes, the schools are below capacity, but they work. She doesn't trust the school system to change things without destroying what's there.

Judy knows that some neighborhood parents haven't liked the existing schools as much as she has and that they hope to enroll their children in one of the new charter schools. But those parents have options in other neighborhoods. Why can't they, and the children from low-performing schools who are likely to enroll in the charters, go someplace else?

Some other mothers have asked Judy to join them in a rally organized by the teachers union against closing schools the district has called low performing. The other mothers reason that if schools aren't closed, there will be no need to move the new charters into the neighborhood. Judy gets the point, but something about it made her uncomfortable, so she decided not to join them.

In all the cities we studied, measures taken in pursuit of better schools have caused controversy, pitting parents who want to exercise choice against neighborhood leaders and service providers who don't want money to leave existing schools. Some applaud local and state leaders' aggressive pursuit of new options. Others abhor the consequences for jobs, traditions, and neighborhood stability, occasionally charging disrespect for local cultures or efforts to dismantle public education.

Did the portfolio strategy cause these conflicts or were they always there? The answer, based on our research, is yes and yes. The conflicts that have arisen in districts pursuing the portfolio strategy were always present in some form, but the portfolio strategy has caused them to flare up.

Public Education's Inevitable Conflicts

Americans have good feelings about public schools. We are all enriched by the sight of little children skipping off to school or returning home to a joyful reunion with parents, by the sound of children's voices at recess, by plays and music performed by high school students, and by stories of teachers' caring and generosity. Public education as a broader enterprise, though, is another matter entirely. Public discussions about K–12 education are seldom sweet or comforting. Conflict is intrinsic to public education for two reasons: first, because children are unable to act in their own interests and must rely on adults to act for them; and second, because no adult group has interests that perfectly match those of children.

This is not to say that adults don't care about children. Parents, teachers, school board members, and even state legislators all care about educating the next generation. They sincerely explain their actions in terms of benefits to children. However, their actions and preferences differ because of their own adult interests. Parents want their children to learn but have other concerns that take time and energy; some also fear losing their children to unfamiliar ideas, places, and careers. Teachers and principals want children to learn, but they have their own families, needs, and preferences, too, which need their attention. Advocacy groups and service providers also have their own interests, including maintaining their funding and reputation for effectiveness. Public figures, including pastors, school board members, mayors, and state legislators, want children to learn but need to manage competing demands and avoid taking actions that might get them cast out of their jobs.

Even though many adult actors sincerely want to act on children's behalf, none is a perfect proxy for a community's children. The result is that different views and interests are constantly being worked out; consequently, public education is never without conflict. A number of conflicts occur so often that the differing views and preferences are extremely well defined. The opposing poles on these conflicts define six intrinsic conflicts of public education, all of which are evident in Yolanda's story.

The first conflict is focus versus responsiveness. Schools have a great deal of work to do in a short time, but there can be many distractions. Public schools must respond to elected officials (school boards, state legislators), bureaucrats at every level of government including the local central office, and the interest groups that know how to use those

> *No adult actor is a perfect proxy for a community's children.*

organizations to advance their agendas. The school day is limited by teachers' contracts, instructional time is reduced so teachers can get mandated training, special subjects are forced into the curriculum, and educators' paperwork burdens increase, as do the number of meetings that administrators must attend. Demands for responsiveness compete directly with the school's core instructional function. Adults often face stronger incentives to do what higher-ups want than what their students need.

The second conflict is local aspirations versus global aspirations. Schools are community institutions that grow out of local norms and expectations. But they are also instruments of state government, which makes attendance compulsory and requires schools to prepare children for a national, not a strictly local, economy. Conflicts between families and schools, schools and their school boards, and local communities and higher authorities can be serious.

The third conflict is common student experience versus differentiation. Schools expose students from different backgrounds to one another, and they try to give all students access to core skills and ideas. But every student comes to school with a unique set of skills, aptitudes, and interests. Somehow schools must balance the common with the distinctive. When does common instruction misuse talent, and when does differentiation deny some students experiences from which they might benefit? Can schools be designed around particular interests or must they all be the same?

The fourth conflict is about emphasis: should it be on only what can be counted or on everything that counts? Growth of student capacities in reading, mathematics, and science is easier to measure and to track than other core skills. Students' test scores in those subjects are valuable because they can identify problems while there is still time to do something about them. Yet reliance on tests can slight other subjects, encourage teachers to teach to the test, and lead outsiders to make incomplete judgments of schools. Conflict between those who would use tests as proxies for overall school performance and those who would not use them at all is inevitable.

The fifth conflict is between generosity and parsimony in public funding. Supporters of generosity value the symbolism of a generous commitment to education and do not think educators should be required to count the cost of everything they do. However, many taxpayers would prefer that public schools cost less rather than more. Some who would rather provide too much than too little still want educators to use money as productively as possible. Even in good times there are limits to funding. In tough economic times legislators and taxpayers, facing real trade-offs, often deny funding that educators believe they need.

The sixth conflict is a closed versus open teaching force. Most adults remember a teacher who changed their lives and hope their children will experience someone similar. However, in the name of encouraging the best teachers to make careers in the profession, the U.S. public education system has offered lifelong job security with little attention to differences in teacher performance. The promise of a lifetime job is justified as a way to make a modestly paid profession more attractive. But this approach has consequences. In surveys, teachers, principals, and parents agree that there are many weak teachers, who constitute problems for students and other faculty members.

Many polls find that Americans hold contradictory views: they believe their teachers and schools to be of high quality but hold a lower opinion of public education in general. A 2003 Public Agenda metasurvey, combining findings from many other surveys, found that 85 percent of parents agree that, in their child's school, most teachers are committed and really care about their students.[1] However, 60 percent of Americans consider teacher quality to be a problem in the nation's schools. In a Gallup Work and Education poll conducted in 2009, less than half of Americans are satisfied with the quality of K–12 education in the United States. "Americans most commonly mention having higher-quality, better-educated, and more-involved teachers as the best way to improve kindergarten through grade 12 education in the United States. The next-most-common public prescription is to focus on a basic curriculum of reading, writing, and arithmetic. Improved funding, better teacher pay, and smaller class sizes also receive a significant number of mentions."[2] There is a serious argument over whether less restrictive licensing and performance-based pay would attract more talented people to teaching.

These conflicts are inherent in public education. It is hard to imagine any way in which an education system for young children featuring taxpayer money and compulsory attendance would not face these challenges in some form.[3] Conflict can become intense under two circumstances: when one or more groups has become aware that public education is not meeting its needs and thinks something can be done about it; and when a proposed change threatens an interest that is already doing very well without the change. Lack of conflict can mean that some groups have accepted half a loaf or have given up for the moment; it never means that all the issues have been resolved.

One connection is consistent: the more pervasive the change the hotter the conflict is likely to become, as interests that are well served under current arrangements become threatened. Changes that do not upset those who are currently well served are possible, but these are unlikely to meet the needs of those who are currently badly served. In the sections below we show how the six conflicts are manifest in all portfolio districts and how portfolio district leaders are—or are not—managing them.

Focus versus Responsiveness

The portfolio strategy takes a strong-schools approach to educational improvement. It strengthens schools at the expense of the traditional central office. It also threatens groups that control schools by influencing this office, including well-established activist groups on many sides of many issues, most important, teachers unions. The portfolio strategy does not deny the importance of curriculum, instructional methods, teachers' qualifications, or professional development. But it considers these subject to improvement at the school level, not something the district manages centrally.

School Autonomy

New York City grants every school control over its spending and hiring, but if the chancellor and his team think a school is not capable of using this autonomy effectively, it is closed. In New Orleans, the recovery school district (RSD) chartered the majority of its schools, using chartering as a framework for guaranteeing schools both freedom of action and a continuation based on performance. Washington, D.C., is far less clear about its grant of autonomy to schools. It expects principals to assemble and lead effective teaching staffs and will fire ineffective principals who don't. Chartering is done by an independent agency, which does not coordinate its actions with DC Public Schools.

Chicago has been inconsistent about schools' freedom of action. Though nearly half of all Chicago schools enjoy some form of autonomy, a nearly equal number are centrally managed just as they were before the mayoral takeover. When it wants to establish autonomy, Chicago uses chartering and many other administratively created arrangements. It also used contracting as a way to establish school autonomy at a time when the Illinois charter law strictly capped the numbers of charter schools. However, contracts proved susceptible to constant reinterpretation by district legal staff and have not guaranteed the desired level of school autonomy.

Buffering School Leaders

Aside from creating well-defined school autonomy, districts pursuing the portfolio strategy also try to minimize the noneducational demands on schools by insulating them from demands unrelated to effective instruction. Of course no strategy can totally remove politics from public education. Still, the portfolio strategy can reduce the number and prominence of forums in which demands are made and can buffer school leaders from pressure to satisfy every demand.

Portfolio districts do these things in different ways. Districts under mayoral or state takeover generally have school boards, but these have limited powers; often they are able only to vote up or down on proposals put before them. Leaders in these districts also discourage highly emotional school board meetings, on the assumption that such forums generate demands that might not be easily met.

Weakening the Traditional Central Office and Its Allies

A smaller, more tightly managed, and less powerful central office bureaucracy limits the number of channels by which influential groups can arrange patronage jobs, contracts, and special treatment. In New York City under Joel Klein, minor elected officials who wanted a person hired or promoted could make their demands only to the chancellor or a member of his leadership team, who would then deny them. This meant that schools were not forced to take unwanted employees or distort their budgets or work assignments to satisfy an external demand. Access points are also limited in New Orleans. Strong executive leadership has also reduced access in Washington and Chicago, though demands still get through via the mayor's political operators.

Portfolio districts with functioning school boards also look for ways of exempting schools from constant scrutiny, using chartering or special flexibility or innovation exemptions from normal governance. Though successful, this buffering function is difficult to perform and requires more constant adaptation and reassertion than in takeover districts.

Opposition

Such arrangements might look good to district and school leaders, but they are far less popular with people who are kept away from those in control. Individual parents can find themselves forced to deal directly with a principal or teacher whom they would prefer to outflank by going to the central office or an elected official. Groups advocating for particular approaches to instruction, or for particular neighborhoods, have fewer (and less compliant) places to take their demands. When schools are buffered from outside pressure, elected officials can find it more difficult to do casework for allies and constituents and, thus, perceive losses in power and in their ability to reward supporters. Some elected officials also oppose the school choice aspects of the portfolio strategy, because it can dilute the connection between living in a constituency and schooling children there. Groups that once took contracts to run particular programs, or to keep the peace in particular neighborhoods, can also feel deprived.

Opposition from groups that once got contracts through the central office can be especially strong. In New Orleans groups that worked for and with the school system before Hurricane Katrina charge that the RSD is deaf to their demands and blind to their value. Former neighborhood groups trying to reestablish their constituencies struggle against the city's choice policy. They charge that city and state powers are deliberately thwarting them. Groups that once received district funding for services, representation, and forum management have also been left out. Most significantly, the local teachers union, which once controlled teachers' employment throughout the city, has been gravely weakened by school-level hiring and by the district's refusal to automatically rehire former New Orleans school district teachers.[4]

> *Closing schools can set the leaders of portfolio districts on a collision course with the families they most want to help.*

Though the new RSD schools employ many African American teachers, and a majority of African American parents report a high degree of satisfaction with their children's schools, virtually all of the left-out teachers and group leaders are African American. This has led to charges that the RSD's limitation of political access is part of a white takeover of the city. Well founded or not, accusations of racial discrimination have increased the fervor of protest against the RSD.

In New York, Klein and his collaborators expected, but were surprised at the virulence of, opposition from neighborhood political figures (including some state legislators). These officials had worked as "fixers" under the old system, getting jobs and contracts for supporters and intervening in the schools on behalf of constituent families. Klein closed off opportunities for "fixing" by eliminating central office employees' abilities to make deals with neighborhood figures. As one leadership team member said, "minor elected officials would call to get someone a job or ask someone in the central office to lean on a principal, and they would be outraged that there was no one able to do what they wanted." As a result, some neighborhood political figures complained that the Department of Education had moved too fast, consulted too briefly, excluded good people from jobs and opportunities for influence, and failed to negotiate actions over which certain individuals had once held veto power.

Americans loathe endless political dickering. Yet they can be sympathetic to claims that decisionmakers did not consult broadly enough. People who come out on the losing side of a public decision often sincerely feel that officials would have acted differently if only they had listened. In districts pursuing the portfolio strategy, the claim of inadequate consultation is inevitable because city leaders deliberately close political theaters and limit opportunities for revisiting decisions. Portfolio district leaders claim with justification that these things are done to protect schools' ability to focus. But counterclaims are inevitable and sometimes are more than plausible.

Such conflicts can only be arbitrated in the court of public opinion or at the ballot box. The most sophisticated leaders of portfolio districts know that they must deal with objectors in ways that third parties (opinion makers and the broader public) consider respectful and competent. As we show in this chapter, this is not always an easy maxim to follow.

Local versus Global Aspirations

More than anything else, leaders of portfolio districts seek to provide better options for families of children stuck in unproductive schools. They think all families should have choices, not just those who can afford to move into neighborhoods with the best schools or pay private school tuition. This belief in family choice does not, however, amount to a commitment to giving parents anything they want or continuing to support any school that families like. To the contrary, leaders of portfolio districts are committed to closing schools they consider harmful, even if families like them, and to offering new options, even if they threaten the financial viability of popular schools.

In taking this view, portfolio district leaders are part of a long tradition in public education of imposing performance standards derived from broad analysis of economic and social trends and assuming that parents don't always understand what their children need to know in order to become successful adults. Frank expressions of this elitist attitude are politically incorrect, but it is a founding premise of public education. The government uses taxpayer money (often collected from reluctant payers) to provide schools and compels parents to send their children to them. It does so on the assumption that many parents could not afford to pay enough for quality education and that some parents would not understand what a child needs to become a full member of the adult community.

School closing can be a consensus function when the schools closed are violent and dangerous. But for schools that are not widely feared, closing can set the leaders of portfolio districts on a collision course with the families they most want to help. When closing a school that parents have not been begging to leave, district leaders essentially say to them that they have been sending children to a school that is harmful to them. This is naturally troubling to parents. It also invites a challenge: either the school district was not doing its job in the past, or it is making a mistake now.

School Closing Dilemma

District leaders who are convinced that they have a responsibility to close a school are in a tough place. Though no school is so popular that some families wouldn't like to get out of it, large numbers of families like most schools, feel good about the teachers, appreciate the extracurricular activities, and don't want to see a local public facility closed. These families are natural allies for teachers who want to preserve their job assignments and for neighborhood politicians and service providers who don't want their constituencies broken up.

School closings have created conflicts in all portfolio districts. In New Orleans, New York, and Denver, charter schools as well as neighborhood schools have been closed for low performance, sparking opposition from prominent citizens, donors, teachers, parents, and school heads. Some school closings, such as Manual High School in Denver, have left a bitterness that still affects the neighborhood. In Washington, which has closed relatively few schools, the firing and replacement of principals and the widespread firing of teachers rated ineffective have set off their own firestorms.

School closing is a form of policy termination, a difficult feat for any public organization. The number of people who might benefit from termination can be large—if for example closing some schools and assigning children to others leads to increases in the number of educated adults.

However, these benefits are shared lightly by large numbers of people, and they can be realized only after a significant time lag. On the other hand, the people who experience harm because of the termination—teachers, parents, neighborhood figures—experience it intensely and immediately. The latter group has much stronger incentives to organize, attend meetings, demonstrate, and threaten public officials than do residents who benefit.

City leaders following the portfolio strategy can decide to slow down school closings and work harder to build support for their actions. But in the long run, if they believe children are being harmed by a school and that the school can't improve dramatically in a short time, they feel an obligation to send students elsewhere. In one city that has been forced by a political backlash to slow the pace of closings, a top leader believes that one in six schools in the district needs to be closed and replaced. But he fears the district can't survive the conflict that would arise from closing more than one in ten. To him, this means the district will be forced to defer doing its duty and fail to help a whole generation of students who pass through these weak schools. Not poking the hornet's nest of a weak school is, in his mind, a dereliction of duty.

Learning Lessons the Hard Way

Leaders in the six cities studied here have all continued closing schools even as they have learned hard lessons. Perhaps the most important lesson is that they must accept the burden of proof, both that a given school is consistently failing its children and that an alternative will serve them better. Evidence about a school's performance relative to that of other schools serving similar children is indispensable. Unfortunately, district leaders have not always had this evidence available. Even when they did, it was often presented in ways that parents could not readily apply to their own children: low overall test scores or proficiency measures. More specific information—for example, the probability that a student in the school will graduate from high school—is probably more helpful to parents.

Leaders have also learned to give parents some time to take in the information that their school needs to be closed. In Oakland, for example, schools likely to be closed are identified nearly twenty months before the possible closing date. A list of schools slated for closing is published nine months before the closures actually happen. Many parents won't be reconciled to the decision even given information and time, but many do come to accept the idea and consider the benefits. Advanced notice can also give political opponents time to organize, an issue we turn to later. Portfolio district leaders have also learned that parents need information about where their children can go once the current school is closed. Chicago's failure to do that explains the abandonment of its Renaissance 2010 initiative more than any other factor.

It is particularly hard to tell parents about their children's next school if the plan is to replace a conventional district-run school with a charter. In New York and New Orleans, charter laws forbid guaranteeing anyone admission to a charter school. Families whose schools are closed can apply to the charter school that replaces it. But if the new school is attractive and parents from across the city also apply, a neighborhood child might lose out in the admissions lottery. Parents need to hedge their bets by also applying to more distant and less familiar schools. Thus parents whose school is closed can lose a known situation only to gain a profoundly uncertain one.

New York City has tried to reduce the dislocation parents feel by closing schools a grade at a time, introducing a new school only at the lowest grade level served, and allowing students to stay in the old school until they complete all the grades offered there. This reduces some parents' anxieties and gives new schools time to develop a grade level at a time. However, families that had always expected to send their children to the old school are deprived of that option, whether or not they can win admission to the new school. Families that decide to leave the old school as soon as it is slated for closure also endure uncertainty about where their children will be placed. Proof of the need to close a school and the value of the alternative that will become available are necessary preconditions to a successful school closing. Even with these conditions in place, conflict is not eliminated entirely, as some parents still remain unreconciled. Moreover, interest groups, teachers unions, and some elected officials have their own reasons for generating conflict and publicity.

The failure of the first reform of Manual High School in Denver—which led its superintendent, Michael Bennet, to close it for one year, then to reopen it on a staged basis, with only a first-year freshman class—met with intense criticism. But it paid off: the dropout rate of the first graduating class of 2011 plummeted, 93 percent of entering freshmen graduated, and 89 percent of them were accepted by colleges.

Teachers unions in particular might realize that a given school will inevitably close but want to deter similar actions in other schools. A major scene, including accusations of district arbitrariness and refusal to consult, might weaken district leaders and make them tread more lightly in the future. A union lawsuit against school closings in New York City in 2010 stopped the closing process for an entire year and required more formal proof and consultation in the future. Leaders of the New York portfolio strategy paid the price of meeting all the requirements and went ahead with an ambitious slate of school closings in early 2011. However, unions mounted major demonstrations, and public consultations were long, heated, unpleasant, and irresistible to television reporters. This all came at a time when Mayor Michael Bloomberg's popularity was in decline and after the mayor had to fire Cathie Black, the person he had designated as Joel Klein's successor. But it is still not clear whether the union in New York City has slowed down the school closing process.

School Closing as a Political Process

New York City has also tried to avoid school closings altogether by requiring underenrolled schools to share their buildings with new schools, often charters. This has removed the need to make a case against a particular school, but it has done little to dampen the conflict. Parents and teachers have risen up to defend their space and have even enlisted an anticharter *New York Times* reporter on their side. The district's effort has run up against school communities' belief that they own their buildings, even when they are provided free by the city and underutilized. In the future, school colocations, which could be ways of improving the supply of schools without the agony of closings, will require new policies, such as rent for the use of facilities beyond a maximum number of square feet per student.

School closing is ultimately a political process. Portfolio district leaders need to build alliances and convince the attentive public that they have acted responsibly and with due consideration for the people most affected. They must expect opposition. They must consult openly, understanding that opponents of a closing decision will always claim that they did not consult enough. They must justify their actions, again making sure that a fair third party would be convinced school closings were necessary. The conflict will not go away. To duck it and allow truly harmful schools to remain open is to put harmony over the interests of children.

Common Student Experience versus Differentiation

In American public education there is always a tension between providing a common educational experience for all and meeting particular needs or developing exceptional talents. Traditional school districts have managed these tensions in two ways: first, by deliberately creating a few schools to cater to unusual tastes or talents and, second, by creating "shopping mall" schools, which try to provide something for everyone.

The portfolio strategy also creates varying types of schools, but it does this as a core strategy, not as an exception. Every school is adapted to some particular need, whether of a neighborhood or of a group of students. This means that questions like, What is common among public schools? and Won't this stratify students by income or ability? come up every time, not just occasionally. The portfolio strategy discourages schools that have vast course catalogs in favor of simpler schools that take a single coherent approach to student motivation and instruction— and do it well. This preference for simpler, more coherent schools is backed by the literature about school effectiveness.[5] It is driven by the budgetary reality that a school can either do a few things very well or many things less well. Schools that do one thing very well (such as emphasize science and mathematics) must often do less of something else (such as student bands or advanced art courses). Parents accustomed to shopping mall schools are often incredulous when they find a particular program is not available; teachers can also be outraged to learn that a public school does not employ anyone from their specialty.

Even with open admissions, some parents feel deprived when a nearby school does not offer everything they want for their child. They are not always glad to know they can get what they want by choosing another school. In New York City, which has closed many large comprehensive high schools and replaced them with a few smaller, more specialized schools, parents fear loss of extracurricular activities and course options. Parents and neighbors often fear a new school and new staff will neglect a local tradition (such as a birthday party for every student, as in the old school in Yolanda's neighborhood). PTAs and neighborhood groups that have paid for improvements to a school building also resent "outsiders" benefiting from such additions as library books, playgrounds, and fencing.

Though the tensions created by school specialization are not as severe as those connected to school closing, they can be serious. Families and neighbors might accept, and even support, a smaller more specialized school. But it might take them years to feel that they know the staff and look at it as a local asset. Schools that appeal to students with particular talents or interests can be criticized for being elite, even if they do not handpick students by income, race, or test scores. Similarly, schools that offer specialized programs for disadvantaged students—such as dyslexic students or English-language learners—can easily be characterized as dumping grounds, even if they meet students' needs well. Claims of these sorts inevitably arise in portfolio districts, and it takes a great deal of attention to staffing, resourcing, and performance tracking to make sure they are not true.

These problems are painfully evident in New Orleans, where the majority of schools, as charters, do not receive special funding or outside services for special education students. With some unfortunate exceptions, New Orleans charter schools accept students with learning disabilities and try to serve them in regular classes with instant remediation for anyone who falls behind. No one—not the individual charters, the RSD, or the state of Louisiana—has yet figured out how to serve high-needs students in schools with defined budgets.

> *Portfolio districts create different types of schools as a core strategy, not as an exception.*

In the future, portfolio districts might have to create innovative risk pools or insurance-like arrangements, whereby all schools pay equally to support special education services for all local students. In the past, the costs of special education could be hidden in the district budget; nobody could calculate how much their school paid for special education or whether other schools paid or got as much as they did. Though schools were in effect taxed, the amounts were hard to estimate, and the funds were never transferred to schools. Charter schools receive cash for the students they enroll and must pay cash for any services those children receive. It is impossible to hide large expenditures that reduce the amounts available for general instruction or other key activities.

By making transparent decisions about school focus and student assignment, portfolio districts make obvious conflicts that were previously hidden. People will disagree about whether it is necessary to stir up so many things that had been settled for a long time. In general, opposition to change comes from those who benefited most from the prior arrangements. In the case of conflicts over elitism versus meeting common needs, portfolio districts have called attention to issues that have been long settled, whether equitably or not.

Where to Place the Emphasis

No one would undertake anything as challenging as a portfolio strategy unless they thought their existing schools were in dire need and felt a change could make a profound difference in students' experience and results. Mayors who have adopted portfolio strategies are particularly eloquent about how their cities' futures depend on an educated population. It is not enough for children just to spend time in school; they must emerge ready for additional education, eventually to become the city's professionals, nonprofit heads, teachers and professors, clergy, interest group leaders, entrepreneurs, and artists.

How do these long-term goals square with portfolio districts' high reliance on short-term results, particularly test scores? Nobody seriously thinks education is only about test scores. Even the most avid proponents of testing believe that tests are merely indicators of more important measures. Tests provide information about whether and what students are learning—and provide it soon enough to rescue students who are falling behind. There are other and far better measures of the results of schooling: high school graduation, college admission, passing college courses without remediation, finding employment, high lifetime income, civic participation. But these are available only after the fact, while test scores can be available immediately.

Opponents of testing seldom acknowledge its unique advantages. Those who do respect testing claim that the timeliness of test scores is more important than the claimed side effects: one such claim is that the curricula narrow to only those topics likely to be tested and leads to the neglect of arts, history, literature, and multicultural understanding. Another claim is that schools serving the poor are left to fail. Thus the conflict: leaders of portfolio districts believe it is necessary to identify schools and students who are in trouble and to do something about them immediately. For this course of action they need testing. Opponents of testing believe that it makes schools weaker and harms students.

To find a middle ground, some portfolio district leaders have combined testing with other student performance indicators, like attendance, normal progress toward graduation, passing key courses, and student effort. On schools' performance, measures are taken of school diligence in remedying students' problems, school climate, and British-style school inspections. Moreover, alert to the problem that test scores are usually lower in schools serving disadvantaged pupils, leaders in Denver, New York, and New Orleans also measure annual rates of student gain compared to students starting at the same achievement level (see chapter 5).

The story of Choir Academy in New York City illustrates the importance of considering—in addition to test scores—a determination and willingness to take on problems. By the time a new principal, A. Ellen Parris, arrived in 2007, Choir Academy was marked for probable closure. The school had been through four or five leaders. The students were traumatized over the loss of the choir (previously run in collaboration with the Boys Choir of Harlem), and the staff felt beaten down. The result was disorder. "The students were more in control of the school than the teachers," Parris said. Slowly, under Parris's leadership, the school began to stabilize. The bad publicity hurt school enrollment but also had the effect of shrinking class size, making it easier to give students individual attention. These days, there are just twenty-five ninth graders, one-third the normal amount, and enough instruments in the school band that every student can sign one out and take it home. The school received a B on its annual report card, giving it a reprieve from closure, and the graduation rate climbed to 70 percent. "We kept faith when the Department of Education was losing faith," said Willie Abercrombie, seventeen, a senior who plans to be an engineer. "The students are doing more for the school now. It's up to us."[6]

Supplementary short-term measures and use of gains as well as score levels have done little to allay the fears of antitesting groups, however. They continue to point out that schools struggling to show gains emphasize materials likely to be tested and spend time on test preparation. These charges are based on examples, not citywide statistics, so it is difficult to know whether the problems identified are common or rare. Nor is it clear whether there was any more ambitious teaching in struggling schools before current testing regimes were introduced or whether schools whose students cannot read should still try to teach such courses as arts, literature, civics, and history.

In the absence of compelling facts on either side, the conflict persists. Portfolio district leaders have the advantage in that laypersons, including business and academic leaders and many parents, are inclined to believe that test results matter. College and university admissions officers continue to care, even those who use other admissions standards that correlate closely with test results. However, inconsistent or undisciplined use of tests—leading for example to dramatic and noncredible changes in a school's performance from one year to the next, as happened in 2009 in New York City—does not help their case. This conflict is likely to continue. It can produce a clear winner only if the consistent use of test scores to close low-performing schools and to open more effective ones proves conclusively to increase ultimate student outcomes, like graduation rates, college admission, and the ability to do college work without remediation.

Generosity versus Parsimony in Public Funding

Education reformers can be put into two groups: those who think the public education system would work well for everyone if only it had more money, and those who think the system needs to be changed whether or not it gets better funding. Low-tax advocates fit into the latter group but so do those who think the system needs to be reengineered for greater productivity.

Portfolio is a fix-the-system strategy. However it is not sold politically as a cost-control strategy. It does cost money, at least to start up new schools and to build new support and accountability organizations.

Money Makes Change Sweeter–for a While

Some portfolio districts have benefited from significant increases in funding. As Leanna Stiefel and Amy Schwartz show, New York's portfolio strategy benefited from a nearly 30 percent increase in money for teacher salaries in the years 2003–08.[7] This made it easier for teachers union leaders to accept—and to survive membership misgivings about—early Klein actions, such as closing schools. The United Federation of Teachers accepted greater school-level control of hiring on this premise. Extra funding also allowed Klein to isolate tenured teachers, whom no school wanted to employ, in "rubber rooms," where teachers spent normal working hours and drew full salaries but had no duties. In the recent fiscal downturn, Klein, unable to fire the rubber room teachers, placed them into schools, despite the fact that school leaders did not want them.

In New Orleans, post-hurricane FEMA money, coupled with federal education department emergency funding, allowed the RSD to repair school buildings, create some new schools in anticipation of students returning to New Orleans, and invest in new charter schools. In Washington, teachers accepted a new contract, giving the chancellor the authority to terminate low-performing teachers in return for dramatic increases in pay for teachers rated as high performing.

Philanthropy also figured heavily. Investments were made in teacher and principal training centers and in new independent school assistance organizations in New York City (the school support networks) and New Orleans (via New Schools for New Orleans).[8] As these sources of extra money dry up, portfolio district leaders will face the problem of sustaining changes without the sweeteners.

Portfolio Strategies Can Survive without Sweeteners

Current fiscal stresses in all districts mean the end of spending increases and the need to cut spending, often via layoffs. Conflict, especially with teachers unions, is likely to become more severe. The 2010 and 2011 teachers union lawsuits against New York City school closings signaled the end—or at least a suspension—of the United Federation of Teachers' cooperation with the Bloomberg regime. But it is not clear that lack of funding will stall development of the portfolio strategy. Some cities with huge deficits, such as Detroit, are looking to a charter-heavy portfolio strategy to develop new schools and hire teachers with less ruinous benefit packages. In other cities (such as Hartford) the portfolio strategy has been sustained on a relative shoestring.

The portfolio strategy is advancing in the absence of dramatic sweeteners (see chapter 6). Aside from the political advantage of new funding, the portfolio strategy can be cost neutral or even save money. But that is possible only if district central office expenditures are eliminated in favor of independent assistance organizations and if local and national philanthropies are willing to sustain customary levels of support and make different use of existing levels of philanthropy. The portfolio strategy needs flexible funds to pay for start-up organizations, including school providers, assistance organizations, district accountability offices, and the reconfiguration of facilities.

If these investments are made on a one-time basis, with permanent operations dependent on money received from taxpayers, it is possible that the portfolio strategy can deliver on the implied promise of improvement through reform, not permanent increases in funding. However, mayors and other leaders in the most prominent portfolio cities have not always been disciplined about segregating short- from long-term funding.

Closed versus Open Teaching Profession

Teaching as a career and vocation is well established in American culture. This was true long before teachers created unions and before formal tenure rights and formal step-and-lane pay structures.[9] Unionization and adoption of civil service–style pay and job security made teaching into an occupation set apart, with strong barriers to entry and the expectation of little or no mobility into and out of other lines of work. There is no real controversy over the desirability of a secure and remunerative career for truly excellent teachers. Everybody remembers a dedicated, mature teacher whose long experience was an asset to everyone they taught.

But portfolio districts come down on one side of the controversy over whether teaching should be a lifetime career for almost everyone who takes a teaching job out of college. Portfolio districts didn't create the controversy, but they are caught up in it. Every portfolio district is experimenting with new ways of attracting teachers, rewarding the best, and winnowing the supply to make room for high-potential new entrants who are not traditional education school graduates. Districts approach this in many ways.

After Katrina, New Orleans recruited a new teaching force, including present and past Teach for America (TFA) members, who made up more than 10 percent of the local teaching force in the 2010–11 school year; a similar number of teachers hired through the New Teacher Project; conventionally trained educators from other parts of Louisiana, other states, and other countries; and former Orleans Parish teachers, who remain the most numerous group. Teachers from all sources work in all RSD schools, but the newest teachers are likely to work in charters. Since the majority of RSD schools are charters, and charters set their own pay scales, the majority of New Orleans teachers receives individually negotiated salaries and can be promoted rapidly. Critics have warned against continuing reliance on TFA corps members, because many leave after two years. But New Orleans continues to attract large numbers of volunteers, and an estimated 15 percent stay in the local schools as teachers and leaders after their two-year stint is complete.

New York has drawn a similar number of TFA and New Teacher recruits, as has New Orleans, and has also built a secondary teaching force among charter school teachers. However, the vast size of the district means that tens of thousands of teachers are still employed in the traditional way and covered by the collective bargaining agreement with the United Federation of Teachers. The district has managed this teaching force via two arrangements: by letting schools refuse to employ experienced teachers who lost positions in other schools and by creating strong incentives for principals not to keep weak teachers until they are automatically tenured. The former arrangement has been popular with principals but has been very expensive, as teachers without posts were still paid, and during the current fiscal crisis district leaders have gone back to forcing school leaders to take some unwanted teachers back into classrooms.[10] The latter arrangement has had a profound effect on the quality of New York teachers, virtually eliminating the weakest part of the teacher talent distribution and reducing the apparent teacher quality gap between teachers in low- and high-income schools.[11]

New York has not fought the principle that teachers who perform well in their first few years can be tenured, but it has tried to raise the quality of those who are granted tenure: first, by rigorously enforcing requirements that teachers must pass challenging qualification tests before they are hired; and second by discouraging principals from granting tenure to teachers whose performance is mediocre. Regarding the latter, principals are evaluated in part on the subsequent performance of teachers whom they allow to gain tenure.

Denver's ProComp teacher pay system was started before Bennet embraced the portfolio district model. It continues to attract teachers from outside the city and to reward the highest performing teachers disproportionately. Denver is also building a secondary teaching force among its growing number of charter schools. Washington, like New York, has tried to recruit teachers from a broader range of backgrounds than before, including experienced teachers from elsewhere on the Eastern Seaboard. It has also developed a widely publicized teacher pay and incentive system, which offers teachers major salary increases for abandoning their tenure rights.[12]

In addition to creating portfolios of schools, portfolio districts have created portfolios of sources of teachers, pay schemes, and terms of employment. None of these portfolios discourages long tenure and high pay for the most outstanding teachers. They all create opportunities for new teachers to advance quickly on the basis of performance and discourage continued employment for less productive teachers. These actions put portfolio districts into conflict with a coalition of interests that have defined teacher qualifications and careers in the past. Both traditional schools of education (gatekeepers to the teaching career) and teachers unions (protectors of teachers once they take jobs in public school systems) can be threatened by a local portfolio strategy.

Though education schools have not been consistent opponents of the portfolio strategy, they have fought for "alternative certification" policies that protect their own stakes as mandatory course providers. Teachers unions have been more active, opposing school closings that threaten members' jobs and the expansion of charter schools that provide wholly different modes of employment for teachers. Unions are also militant in opposing a linkage of teacher pay to student test score gains, though Denver and Washington teachers have voted for contracts that include elements of what is called performance-based pay. These pay schemes are not inevitable elements of the portfolio strategy: New Orleans, New York, Chicago, Baltimore, and Hartford either leave existing pay schemes alone or allow school leaders to set pay based on their perceptions of value to the school. But Washington and Los Angeles have pressed hard for teacher pay schemes that use measurements of student gains as weighty elements of a teacher pay formula.

"Safer" reforms that did not threaten anyone have had little effect.

It is not yet clear whether centrally managed performance pay schemes like the one in Washington are compatible with other elements of a portfolio strategy: when pay is set centrally by formula, school leaders lose freedom of action. Some fear that teachers, knowing that the school head can't shield them from the consequences of a low student gain score, will avoid tough assignments. These provisions might prove to be incompatible with the school autonomy elements of the portfolio strategy. In Los Angeles as in Washington, district leaders seem willing to trade school

BOX 4-1. United Federation of Teachers and the Chancellor of the Board of Education

Relations between the United Federation of Teachers and Joel Klein, chancellor of the board of education, have been extremely complex. In 2006 the UFT agreed to operate a charter campus with a middle and elementary school in East New York. But while going along with parts of Klein's reform strategy, the UFT criticized the strategy as a whole. Furthermore, the union did not support Mayor Bloomberg's candidacy for a third term in 2009 or Klein's campaign to increase the number of charter schools allowed in New York State. In 2010 the UFT supported a lawsuit that led to substantial regulation of the school-closing process, and it mobilized strong public opposition to the school closings sought in 2011.

autonomy and an open new schools strategy for teacher contracts that they think will make the traditional system work better.

Leaders in New York and Denver are considering a less mechanical use of student gain scores, as part of a package of information provided to school heads and teachers, to be used in school-level decisionmaking. As this is written it is not clear whether this idea will be tried, or how it will work. One thing is certain, portfolio districts will continue to spark conflict in teacher recruitment, assignment, tenure, and school-level discretion over pay and work assignments. These conflicts are likely to become more severe as districts increase the numbers of KIPP-like schools, which require teachers to work longer hours and more days and to experiment with hybrid schools (which deliver some instruction via online technologies and therefore employ fewer teachers; see chapter 2 on New York City's iZone). These developments, which unions seem able to slow down but not to block entirely, are likely to accelerate under today's combination of increased pressure for performance and decreased per-pupil funding. (For an account of the relationship between the United Federation of Teachers and Joel Klein, see box 4-1.)

The Right Amount of Conflict

Conflict is not good in itself, only as a necessary means to achieving something important. Unnecessary conflict, including that caused by indiscriminate action or polarizing rhetoric, generates avoidable opposition. Most leaders of portfolio strategies have tried to avoid gratuitously causing conflict. But they find it, as Chicago's 2012 teachers strike demonstrates. Big changes in the ways time and money are used, what is protected, and what is made contingent are sure to stir conflict. Other, "safer," reforms that do not question or threaten anyone (such as site-based management and standards not linked to performance accountability) have had little effect.

The six conflicts discussed in this chapter are inherent in any situation where people other than parents pay for education and are paid to teach children. Participants naturally characterize such conflicts in ways that are favorable to their own positions: the needs of children versus employees, economic elites versus ordinary people, optimization versus solidarity, neighborhoods versus city hall. Academic theorists add their own twists on such characterizations. Portfolio-style reforms have been called neoliberal, corporatist, and associated with shock doctrine (under which predatory business interests use crises to weaken public institutions and cut businesses in on the use of taxpayer funds).[13] A more neutral formulation is called regime theory, which interprets such strategies as products of public-private coalitions that come episodically together around significant problems, sometime but not always to the disadvantage of groups representing disadvantaged minorities.[14] Charles Sabel's theory of democratic experimentalism provides a positive theoretical framing, characterizing such reforms as ways to support grassroots innovation to solve previously unsolved problems.[15]

All of these academic framings—including those that differ in the moral slant they take—cite many of the same facts but interpret them differently. They provide useful ways of comparing the portfolio strategy with other methods of public decisionmaking, but none can be strictly proven valid except by profound analysis of the thinking of those involved. As we suggest above, the people who lead portfolio strategies are pragmatic and often informed by their own professional experience (such as Joel Klein and Tom Boasberg). Portfolio district leaders might have heard of academic theories and even know the people who formulated them, but that does not mean they are following anyone's blueprint. The same is true of union leaders, parents whose schools are threatened with closure, and elected representatives who don't want school choice to break up their constituencies: they oppose the portfolio strategy because of the risks and costs it imposes on them, not because it fits into some broad theory of politics or social action.

Portfolio district leaders must assume that others working in education want to do well for children, whether or not they have succeeded. Thus respect for opponents and clear explanations of what is done and why are ways to avoid needless strife. Aggressive and consistent communication, about criteria for action and the consequences for different groups of children, is necessary.[16] Communication is also necessary to maintain the support of interested third parties who favor school improvement but are not directly affected by the changes in question. These are the ultimate balance holders, and they need to believe that leaders are competent, decent, and driven by the desire to improve education, not to beat opponents or settle scores.

Unfortunately, no portfolio district leader knows exactly how far he or she needs to go to make dramatic improvements in children's learning and school completion rates. How many schools must be opened or closed and how quickly? How many teachers and principals can adapt to new demands for continuous improvement, and how many cannot? How rapidly can better school providers, principals, and teachers be found to replace the least productive? Nobody can know these answers a priori. Facing these uncertainties and the high stakes for children who are not now in effective schools, portfolio district leaders will often choose a more aggressive, and therefore a higher conflict, course over a conservative one. The prospects, in a naturally conflict-laden environment, for a portfolio strategy to be sustained long enough to be effective, are assessed in chapter 6.

CHAPTER FIVE

Judging the Results of the Portfolio Strategy

Andrea attends the Harlem Success Academy in New York City, and her mother is delighted. It is safer, more peaceful, and more focused on learning than any of the New York City elementary schools her older children attended. Andrea's mother is very upset when she hears the school condemned as harmful to her neighborhood. Many of her neighbors turned out recently to demonstrate against a proposal to let Harlem Success take over an unused part of a nearby school building. She is sure that if other parents knew how good the school was they would be clamoring to get their children in, not block its expansion.

Andrea's mother wishes there were some simple proof of what she feels, that the new schools are much calmer, more focused on what children need to learn, and more effective than the other schools in the neighborhood. Every now and then the Department of Education will put out a report showing how much students are learning. But soon an opposition group puts out another report, drawing the opposite conclusion.

She asks, "Does it have to be this confusing?"

Assessing Portfolio Strategy Results

The portfolio strategy is a complex intervention in an even more complex system. Everything is done in the name of increasing student achievement, but some of the actions taken, though arguably causally connected to student achievement, are remote from it. For example, giving principals control over money and hiring, and a new districtwide talent strategy, contribute to student achievement, but only indirectly. To complicate matters further, some elements of the portfolio strategy that are causally close to student achievement (such as replacing failed schools with new ones or rewarding principals and teachers for high performance) might produce the desired results for students in some cases but not in others. A portfolio strategy in any city will take some time to take root and show effects in student performance.

Asking the Right Questions

Citizens and elected officials who want to judge a given city's portfolio strategy will be tempted to cut the Gordian knot by using simple aggregate indicators, such as growth in student scores on state tests or growth in districtwide graduation rates. Gross indicators like these are easy to compute and communicate, and they will undoubtedly be used. However, they can easily mislead. A city that is enjoying an economic boom can gain large numbers of higher achieving students and enjoy a boost in its test score averages all unrelated to the effectiveness of its portfolio strategy. The opposite can be true, too: a district's student population can become poorer and more educationally challenged due to the inmigration of poor families or the departure of better-off families.

Aggregate measures can also hide unequal improvement across a city's neighborhoods or groups of students. A district may post remarkable overall gains by bringing up the bottom of the distribution, an admirable outcome. But that opens up the question of whether achievement levels for more advantaged students have declined. More refined analysis that examines changes in outcomes, such as test scores or graduation rates among identified populations of students, can be more informative (box 5-1).

People are accustomed to tracking changes in student outcomes (such as test scores and completion rates) for particular schools. But the choices created by portfolio strategies can lead to dramatic changes in who attends a particular school. New schools opened in existing buildings can keep the old school's name yet serve very different students. Schools that remain open can lose students to new schools and gain students from schools that are closed. Thus changes in average outcomes in a school can be due to demographic changes: a given school's rise or fall in test scores can be due to a different intake of students. A school that serves a more

---

B O X 5 - 1 .   Outcomes that Matter to Parents and the Community

Student outcomes

Graduation rates: earning an accredited diploma by the end of twelfth grade.

On-track course taking: completing the courses and credits for on-time graduation.

Academic growth: ongoing progress in standardized assessment.

District outcomes

High-performing seats: availability of seats in high-performing schools.

Improved teacher quality: fewer emergency certified teachers, higher preservice exam scores, improved teacher retention.

Equitable outcomes

Consistency of outcomes across the district's neighborhoods and student populations.

---

disadvantaged population as a result of the portfolio strategy could improve the outcomes for the students now attending it, yet show a decline in average scores compared to an earlier time.

Although district administrators and newspapers will inevitably discuss outcomes in particular schools, definitive judgments about the effectiveness of the portfolio strategy requires tracking changes for individual students. A bottom-line judgment on the portfolio strategy depends on answers to questions such as:

—Did the students who attended newly established schools benefit?

—Were students in schools slated for closure facing long odds of success before closure? Did their odds of success improve after the closure?

—In cases where schools were slated for closure but remained open for a while, which students stayed until the end? Did these students benefit or suffer academically from staying in the to-be-closed schools?

—How have preexisting schools changed in light of the new school autonomy, student choice, and less centralized support ushered in by the portfolio reforms? How have their student bodies changed? And have their students kept pace with the performance of new schools?

—Are students across the district and of all backgrounds getting access to better teachers and principals?

—Did the school system improve for families of all backgrounds and across the district?

Reformers and critics who want to know what the portfolio strategy in their city has and hasn't accomplished cannot escape the need to look at the results of its key parts. The same is true of city and district leaders who want to know what part of their strategy needs attention.

Answering the Questions

These questions are not easy to answer, and results might be mixed. For example, researchers examining New York City's transition to small high schools find that, while students in small high schools benefited from the reform, those in comprehensive schools found themselves in more crowded circumstances and with more high-needs classmates.[1] If someone simply compares New York City students in new small high schools to those in traditional large high schools, without accounting for changes in traditional schools' student bodies caused by the reform, they would probably overestimate the relative effectiveness of small high schools.

The reforms move students around the system but not necessarily in predictable patterns. Students who previously attended a closed school don't all transfer to the same school or all attend the new school that was put into its place. Students enrolling in new schools will have previously attended a wide variety of schools. To assess their portfolio strategies, cities need good multiyear data on every student, including students' background characteristics, attendance rates, residence, all schools attended, test scores, and courses taken, passed, and failed. More advanced cities are developing such databases, but many are far from perfect and present challenges to analysis.

Once the right data are available, the challenge is comparing actual outcomes to estimates of what would have happened to students in the absence of the portfolio strategy. Thus for a student who moves to a new school, the question is whether his outcomes are better or worse than they would have been in his neighborhood school. Since the latter outcome cannot be observed directly, analysts must estimate what it would have been. This estimate can be arrived at by comparing the student's scores with a those of similar students who did not switch schools or by comparing the rate at which the same student's outcomes improved in the years before versus the years after switching to the new school. These analyses are complex and always imperfect, but they can be—and in some localities, like New York City and Chicago, are starting to be—done.

Six Critical Analyses for Portfolio Districts

Derived from the questions raised at the beginning of this chapter, we frame six critical analyses that, taken together, constitute a proof strategy for a portfolio district (table 5-1). The complexity of the portfolio strategy, however, means that no one analytic approach will be perfect. Three possible analytic approaches are shown in box 5-2.

Portfolio district leaders will also need to provide evidence on local "hot button" issues. In New York City one hot-button issue is colocation of schools, where interest groups have filed suit to block the district's practice of accommodating new schools by placing them in underutilized buildings occupied by district schools. City leaders need to supplement the core proof strategy with an analysis of colocation and its effects on students in schools now asked to share space. In New Orleans, where the accommodation of special education students led to considerable conflict (and now a lawsuit), the RSD needs to analyze the experience of special education students and present this evidence to the public.

As of this writing, neither city has the data and analytic methods necessary to provide all the evidence demanded. It is ironic that a reform strategy that involves data on school assessment would not closely track its effects on the very students whose fortunes it most sought to improve. But this is not new. People with education reform ideas as diverse as class-size reduction, intensive teacher retraining, vouchers, and charter schools consistently assume that the results will be so dramatic that everyone will readily see them. Alas, no reform is strong enough or consistently implemented enough to create unambiguous results in a short period of time. This is particularly true of a continuous improvement approach, like the portfolio strategy, which is built on the expectation of at least a moderate incidence of failure.

There are aggregate results for every city, usually showing that city test scores are improving relative to some standard, whether past performance in the same city or scores elsewhere. In 2011 the Cowen Institute at Tulane University issued its fourth annual report, showing steady overall improvement in students' achievement and persistence in school throughout New Orleans, with the greatest gains for students in new charter schools created after Hurricane Katrina.[2] A+ Denver, a reform support organization, shows that student gains were greatest in the lower income

TABLE 5-1. Six Critical Analyses for Assessing Portfolio Results

	Statistical evidence
Benefits to students who attend new schools	—Students moving from a traditional program to a new program show improved academic gains, such as higher test scores, higher graduation rates, steeper growth trajectories, and greater odds of staying on track than similar students who remained in traditional programs.
	—Analytic strategy: natural experiment with school lottery.
Likely results of not closing the schools that were closed	—Low predicted odds of high school graduation and on-track indicators based on outcomes for current students.
	—Analytic strategy: simulate the predicted odds of staying on track and graduation based on historical trends and compared with current trends.
Impact of closure on students in the school at the time of closure	*Phaseout strategy:* —Improved outcomes (odds of graduation, student academic growth, and on-track indicators) for students who remain during phaseout.
	—Improved outcomes for students who transfer to another school during phaseout.
	Immediate transition: —Outcomes improve after closure or restart.
	—Analytic strategy: time series, comparison to like students for graduation analysis for all above analyses.
Benefits to students who were spared closed schools	—Better outcomes for student who, due to traditional attendance zones and historic attendance patterns, likely would have attended a now-closed school compared with students who attended the closed school.
	—Analytic strategy: comparison to like students.
Benefits to all city students and to those in targeted neighborhoods	—Increased overall graduation rate, increased student achievement in tested grades and subjects.
	—Increased number of high-performing seats both citywide and in affected neighborhoods.
	—Lower achievement gaps between key demographic groups of students.
	—Analytic strategy: district-level time series.
Consequences for the effectiveness of the teacher and principal corps	—Higher average scores on state teacher tests.
	—High-scoring teachers more evenly distributed among the city's schools.
	—Increased teacher and principal retention.
	—Analytic strategy: time series.

BOX 5-2. Three Analytic Approaches

The complexity of the portfolio strategy means that no one approach will be perfect. The three approaches described here represent the most reasonable strategies for responding to the critical analyses discussed.

Natural experiments provided by lotteries. Lottery assignments mimic many of the principles of random assignment for the purpose of assessment. Often, new schools and charter schools are oversubscribed, and slots are filled at random through lotteries. Districts can exploit lottery placements to assess the performance of these new or charter schools by comparing students who "win" the lottery to those who didn't. Analyses based on lotteries are limited in that they can be performed only on oversubscribed schools; many schools, including those about to be closed, are not oversubscribed. In addition, impact assessments derived from comparing lottery winners with losers might not be generalizable to students who did not enter the lottery at all. Thus most districts will have to use other methods in addition to natural experiments.

Time series. Examining patterns over time allows districts to see how students' performance shifts after some shock (such as a school closure) in their schooling. How did the students' performance change after their school was slated for closure? Good time-series analysis requires multiple years of data before and after the shock, which can be difficult to obtain for students early and late in their educational careers. A time series is of no use in examining outcomes that happen just once, such as graduation.

Comparison to like students. Given the data requirements and limitations of natural experiments and time series, districts will need to rely substantially on fabricated comparisons between students. At times students whose academic paths diverge after a specific event can be observed. When a school is phased out, some students may stay while others transfer. When it is time to select a middle school, some students will opt for one in the neighborhood, while others will opt for a charter school. Comparisons between these different paths are inadequate, because we can reasonably assume that some unobserved but likely important trait about the student is behind these different decisions. There will be times when these comparisons are the best that can be done. Statistical matching methods (such as propensity-score matching) and regression models that control for student, school, and community factors provide more suitable comparisons. These methods at least ensure that students with similar backgrounds are compared. Still, the results of these analyses should be interpreted with caution. In general, we would not be able to say convincingly that attending the charter school "caused" the differences we might observe in outcomes (though we could suggest that attending the charter school rather than the zoned school seems related to a difference in outcomes, a nuanced but important distinction).

regions of the city, where new charter schools and closure of low-performing schools were most prevalent.[3] Similar rough comparisons are published from time to time in other cities. These provide talking points for portfolio district leaders but are far from definitive, as analysts using different data and assumptions can often get contrary results.

National organizations using considerably more rigorous methods get similar results for New York and New Orleans. For example, the Rand Corporation's findings on the effectiveness of New Orleans schools post-Katrina are positive, though more hedged than those reported by the Cowen Institute.[4] Stanford University's CREDO also singles out New York and New Orleans charter schools as unusually high performing.[5] The Consortium on Chicago School Research has published a very careful study of test score trends in that city, showing consistent progress over three eras of reform since 1989, despite very low rates of progress for African American students.[6] The authors are careful to avoid strong causal claims, but they note that the portfolio reform and its predecessors are the likeliest causes.

These studies provide plausible backing for portfolio district leaders, who need to show some evidence of progress and even to describe unsolved problems. But simple comparisons of change rates in different jurisdictions are inherently ambiguous about cause and effect: changes in enrollment or student characteristics can make a city look better or worse than its surrounding state, regardless of whether schools are getting better or worse. Though the RAND, CREDO, and Chicago Consortium studies were extremely well done, in some cases the results of aggregate achievement trends can depend as much on what the analyst wants to prove, whether pro or con the portfolio strategy, as on the data.[7]

An Overview of Studies

States and localities are building the kinds of longitudinal, student-based data systems necessary for the analyses we suggest here. Some cities, notably New York and Chicago, are creating the capacity to do needed analyses and have commissioned studies that answer key questions. This section shows fine-grained results from all the cities covered by this book.[8]

New Schools

In a randomized trial in New York, high school students after one year in new small high schools were 10 percentage points more likely to be on track to graduate than those enrolled in other New York City schools.[9] They were 7 percentage points more likely to graduate, which is roughly one-third the size of the gap in graduation rates between white students and students of color in New York City.[10] Graduation rate benefits were sustained for at least five years after the schools opened.[11] Further, students attending new charter schools tested higher than students who applied to the same schools but lost in an admissions lottery.[12]

The typical student in a New York City charter school learned more than similar students in the city. Black and Hispanic students enrolled in charter schools did significantly better in reading and math than their counterparts in traditional public schools. No benefits were shown, however, for English language learners or for special education students.[13] For New York's School of One, which individualizes instruction via technology, there was a mixture of positive and negative outcomes.[14]

In Louisiana, students in charter elementary schools (mostly located in New Orleans) were more likely to make gains than similar students in regular schools.[15] In Chicago, students who transferred to new charter schools that included high school had higher ACT scores and were more likely to graduate and enroll in college than students attending regular Chicago high schools.[16] Students in new charter elementary schools, however, did not learn at a higher rate than when they were in regular schools. There were no consistent differences in test scores between students in new high schools created under the Renaissance 2010 initiative and similar students in existing schools.[17]

These findings, especially for charter schools in New York and New Orleans, are more positive than the findings for new schools nationwide. No one can say for sure why new charter schools in portfolio districts have higher rates of success than charter schools nationwide, but the advantages of district support, equal per-pupil funding, careful selection of charter providers, and the use of available district facilities are obvious.

School Closings

There is essentially no evidence about what would have happened to students who would have attended closed schools had those schools been allowed to remain open. New York City high schools slated for closure had a 43 percent graduation rate, as opposed to 57 percent for other city high schools.[18] New York City often closes high schools one grade at a time and allows incumbent students to complete their studies in their original school. Tables released by the NYC Department of Education show that students who stayed in to-be-closed schools benefited.[19]

In Chicago students forced to leave closed schools suffered some achievement declines in the year after transferring (losing between a half a month and more than a month of progress in reading and math).[20] These losses were regained, on average, in the next year, but this depended on the quality of the next school the student attended: students transferring to higher performing schools benefited from the move. Echoing the results from Chicago, a 2011 Rand study in an unnamed urban district also finds that students transitioning from closing schools saw a temporary dip in performance unless they went on to attend a higher-performing school than the one that closed.[21]

Benefits of Reform

In Chicago students experienced continual achievement growth over the twenty years of reform, although African American students benefited least.[22] The New Orleans charter schools that have opened since Hurricane Katrina have both high test scores and high student persistence.[23] Further, the charter schools operated by the RSD show higher student gains than its traditional schools.[24] In New York City, fourth grade and eighth grade test scores for reading (according to the New York City Department of Education) increased at nearly twice the rate as test scores for the same grades in the rest of the state.

Other signs of the effectiveness of reform show in teacher and principal effectiveness. In New York City, teacher quality increased, nor was there any longer a quality disparity between teachers serving advantaged and disadvantaged students.[25] Schools with principals who were part of the New York City Aspiring Principals Program outpaced schools whose principals were not part of that program.[26] These principals were on average placed in schools whose performance had been declining; three years after the new assignments, reading scores improved.[27] Reform also brought a slight lessening of teacher attrition.[28]

Data from New Orleans also support the conclusion that the new reform strategies have an effect on the teacher corps. In 2011 teachers certified through the New Teacher Project's teachNOLA (a teacher-training program that partners with the RSD) helped raise students' mastery of several subjects, including science, math, and language arts.[29]

Measuring the Effects of the Portfolio Strategy

On balance, measures of portfolio strategy effects in New York City are positive, though the methods used to measure these gains are often very simple and do not carefully factor in demographic changes. Evidence that the talent initiative is having a positive impact on the quality of teachers and school leaders is emerging.

In Washington, New Orleans, Denver, and Chicago there is evidence that the pool of teachers and administrators has improved dramatically due to talent strategies that seek individuals from alternative preparation programs and other localities. However, there is no direct evidence yet that the new recruits are consistently more effective than those they replaced. (As is obvious, there is a great deal more evidence on student outcomes in Chicago and New York City, which both have independent, university-based research institutions dedicated to analysis of K–12 reforms, than in the other cities we studied.)

There is not enough valid information to draw a definitive conclusion about the effectiveness of any city's portfolio strategy. New York City's results, which are the most extensive, are consistently positive but still incomplete. The data suggest that results are modestly positive, with some important exceptions. For example, students in new schools seem to benefit, while students in closed schools can be hurt unless they have extremely good alternative placements.

If (and we emphasize if) full results were available for a city, and they were all highly positive, city leaders and even initially skeptical citizens would have reason to continue supporting the portfolio strategy. If all the results were negative, or even if they were negative on key points such as benefits of new schools, benefits to students spared a closed school, or benefits to students in targeted neighborhoods, it is likely that city leaders and even supporters of the portfolio strategy would be looking for a dramatically different approach. In the real world, however, results are likely to be less clear-cut. What if the results were positive except for students who were in a school when it underwent a closure or a phaseout? In this case, the district needs to be prepared to consider new ways (such as an infusion of resources and expanded options) to protect students who will go through a closure experience.

Even more mixed results—for example, zero benefits for particular neighborhoods, or fewer high-quality teachers in high-poverty schools— would have unpredictable consequences, depending on local politics. Leaders of the local portfolio strategy, however, will almost assuredly be challenged to show that they understand what caused the negative results and have a plausible remedy.

In the end, a complex "scorecard" that zeros in on students can focus debate and the district's decisionmaking, but it cannot take politics out of the way results are perceived. Positive results can weaken critics, just as negative results can strengthen them. However, using a results framework ensures that the portfolio strategy will be judged on what it set out to do, not something else.

As in the case of every education reform idea tried at scale (outside the direct control of the reform's originators), the effects of the portfolio strategy elude easy measurement. Excellent results for a particular student or school make good press, but they are often countered by other examples. In education, as in other fields, weak studies, and even compelling but carefully selected anecdotes, can get as much attention as the most valid statistical report. Members of the public can't tell whether results on one extreme or the other are typical or rare. It is easy to understand why leaders of portfolio districts were in too much of a hurry to arrange rigorous progress assessments. However, nearly eleven years after the reform started in New York City, eight years after Katrina, nine years after Michael Bennet became Denver's leader, and seven years after Michelle Rhee became the school chancellor of Washington, not one of these districts can provide a comprehensive assessment of its own results.

There are valuable results here and there, enough to suggest that the results of rigorous studies could be on balance positive. Portfolio leaders often say they wish they had such evidence, but other priorities inevitably intrude. But to date, portfolio strategies have survived demands for proof in all of the cities we focus on.

Of course, no one can say what will happen the next time opponents claim that the pain of school closures and other changes outweighs the benefits to students.

Does the Portfolio Strategy Have Legs?

Yolanda's mother and father still worry about her schooling: What will happen when she leaves eighth grade and searches for a high school? They hear that many of the noncharter high schools started after Katrina are much like the old New Orleans schools. They want better for her. They worry about the recession and wonder whether the end of the hurricane recovery money will mean that the best teachers will leave, and the schools will be forced to end their tutoring programs and extra-long school day.

The pastor worries too. Professionals in his congregation who favor the change in schools are complaining that the state has overlooked African American businesses in awarding contracts for legal and accounting work. He hopes that isn't true and sees possible trouble ahead. He doesn't want to be seen as one who supported state and national "reformers" rather than standing up for his own people. The pastor also hopes the city can increase the numbers of native-born New Orleans teachers, even while attracting talented teachers and leaders from across the country; but he fears that hiring might flip-flop from one extreme to the other.

Yolanda's parents and their pastor were worried early in 2011 when the two people most identified with the new schools in New Orleans left their jobs. However, they think that the new Recovery School District (RSD) superintendent, Patrick Dobard, seems smart and decent. He is from Louisiana, African American, and obviously determined to keep improving the schools.

In the meantime, Yolanda is happy that her family is back together, that she has good friends in school, and that the teachers are nice and interesting. She knows that her parents are worried about a lot of things, including her transition to high school. But for her that is months away, too far off into the future to worry about.

No gambling houses make book on the likely success of any large-scale school reform initiative. If anyone did, they would have to give long odds. As Rick Hess noted in his 1998 study, few districtwide reform initiatives survive the tenure of the superintendent who introduced them.[1] Most initiatives are doomed by the barely three-year tenure of the average city superintendent. The fact that many big initiatives become dead letters as soon as opposition starts to gather suggests that large-scale reforms face the prospect of a short-term life.

In addition, portfolio strategies can open up previously dormant conflicts and threaten groups that had long been happy with what they got out of the local public school system. So it is no surprise that many observers predict the quick demise of portfolio reforms as soon as the key person (mayor or superintendent) leaves the scene—or even sooner. As we have seen, even New York's chancellor, Joel Klein, and his close associates thought they might have only three to five years to prove the success of their portfolio strategy.

> *Large-scale reforms always face the prospect of a short-term life.*

Portfolio Districts That Are Moving Along

Relative to these expectations, the strategy has proven extremely hardy. Though political leaders know that any public enterprise always is just one misstep away from disaster, portfolio strategies in the cities studied here have survived transitions that looked lethal in prospect.

New York's strategy survived its first expected crisis point, the end of Michael Bloomberg's expected eight years, when the mayor narrowly won a third term. It survived an equally threatening transition when Joel Klein voluntarily resigned the chancellorship and was replaced by Cathie Black, who did not catch on quickly as leader. Her replacement by Dennis Walcott stabilized the reform, even as it faced fresh opposition from the United Federation of Teachers (UFT) and the National Association for the Advancement of Colored People (NAACP) for proposed school closures.

New Orleans is pursuing its portfolio strategy as aggressively under the new RSD superintendent, Patrick Dobard, and the state superintendent, John White. The departures of post-Katrina leaders (the RSD head, Paul Vallas, and the state superintendent, Paul Pastorek) appear to have made the New Orleans reforms less controversial across the state. In addition, state board elections in late 2011 further strengthened political support for the RSD.

In Denver, neither Michael Bennet's departure for the U.S. Senate and his replacement by Tom Boasberg nor the election of a slate of antiport-folio school board members was enough to derail Denver's strategy. Denver elected a new mayor, who is as positive about the reforms as was the former mayor, John Hickenlooper (now Colorado's governor), creating hope that the current narrow school board majority in favor is enough to support the strategy. A school board election in late 2011 provided Boasberg with yet another narrow victory, and he maintains his majority.

Hartford's commitment to the portfolio strategy is strong under the new superintendent, Christina Kishimoto, despite the retirement of the founding superintendent, Stephen Adamowski, the ouster and jailing of Eddie Perez, the mayor who recruited Adamowski, and instances of obstruction by the new mayor, Pedro E. Segarra.

Chicago's commitment to the portfolio strategy flagged after Arne Duncan left to become secretary of education and Mayor Daley appointed a placeholder superintendent. However, Rahm Emanuel, the new mayor, first appointed Jean-Claude Brizard, who had worked on the portfolio strategy in New York City and introduced it to Rochester. His second appointee, Barbara Byrd-Bennet, had served under Duncan. Together, they have introduced a portfolio strategy that is much more ambitious than Duncan's much more circumscribed Renaissance 2010 plan.[2]

Some cases are more difficult to interpret. In Los Angeles, where Chancellor Ramon Cortines introduced the portfolio concept and recruited key senior district staff from other portfolio districts, his successor John Deasy renewed the district's declared commitment to the idea. However, Deasy also pushed hard for a centralized teacher assessment and accountability system and bargained away much of the anticipated creation of new charter schools in order to gain agreement on a collective bargaining agreement that allowed performance-based teacher evaluation and pay. Los Angeles is still opening some new schools but now favors internal new starts that are covered by the union contract. It is still too soon to say how aggressively Los Angeles is pursuing the portfolio strategy, as Deasy seeks to build new partnerships with charter operators. However, it is clear that any shift in strategy resulted from Deasy's own priorities and not from an inability to sustain the portfolio strategy after Cortines's departure.

Washington is the one city in which a reform leader's departure was involuntary. However, the decisive rejection of Washington's mayor Adrian Fenty's reelection bid, fueled at least in part by African American voters' dislike of Michelle Rhee, was not enough to reject Rhee's initiatives. Instead, with strong middle-class support, especially from areas of the city "west of the (Rock Creek) park," the new mayor, Vincent Gray, tapped Rhee's closest collaborator, Kaya Henderson, to be chancellor.

Henderson has pressed ahead with Rhee's agenda, which from the beginning amounted to following two strategies at once. Like Los Angeles, Washington has pursued both central assessment and pay incentives for teachers and portfolio management, but it seems more committed to the former. Though new schooling options are being developed, most of that work is being done outside the official DC Public Schools; instead these options are being developed by the independent District of Columbia Public Charter School Board and a federally funded voucher program. Chancellor Henderson has proposed that DC Public Schools start chartering new schools—a function it abandoned in 2004 after a series of scandals and school failures—but she hasn't yet received the authority.

Keys to Survival

There are good reasons why the portfolio strategy has proven hardier than most other districtwide initiatives. One thing is certain: it hasn't survived because no one opposed it. To the contrary, as previous chapters note, formidable groups have stoutly stood in opposition to it.

Teachers unions in New York and New Orleans have tried to cripple the strategy via lawsuits. In 2010 and 2011, in New York City, the UFT joined with the NAACP to oppose the closure of some low-performing schools and the placement of new charter schools in partly vacant buildings now occupied by existing schools (colocation). Plaintiffs won a 2010 court order demanding a more structured and open process for school closing; but they were rebuffed by the court in 2011 when they tried to reverse school closing and colocation decisions that had followed the court's mandates. In 2012 the union sued to block the district's move to use internal process to restaff (but not literally close or charter out) twenty-six schools; it won in arbitration.

In New Orleans, teachers employed in the city schools pre-Katrina but not rehired sued for back wages and punitive damages. In 2012 a trial judge ruled for the teachers. Both the New York arbitration finding and the New Orleans judge's ruling are now being appealed. In the New Orleans case, the real outcome will come after two cycles of appeal, in the Louisiana Supreme Court. Such litigation is likely to continue and might spread to other localities. Other threats to sustainability include opposition from both state legislators who oppose programs that let families choose schools outside fixed electoral districts and parents in middle-class neighborhoods who do not want their school catchment zones changed. Opposition from low-income families and neighbors also arises in neighborhoods where, as under Chicago's Renaissance 2010, students from closed schools do not have good options.

Test-cheating scandals have flared up in Washington and New York City and also in cities (such as Atlanta) that have tried to avoid pursuing a portfolio strategy. These events have emboldened those who oppose any use of tests to identify low-performing schools or to judge teacher performance. Some claim that performance measurement of any kind inevitably corrupts instruction and, by implication, teachers. However, it is not clear that test cheating is any more common than cheating in any field where money is at stake and workers can readily falsify results. These scandals—and the lack of reasonable test security measures that underlie them—undermine the legitimacy of public education in general and threaten any reform strategy that relies on frequent measurement of results.

The current fiscal crisis also threatens portfolio strategies by reducing funds for investment in new schools, eliminating raises as bargaining chips in union negotiations, and causing layoffs that disproportionately affect new district-run schools with their many junior teachers. In New York City, the fiscal crisis also forced the district to close its "rubber rooms." This forced school leaders, who had been accustomed under the Bloomberg-Klein reforms to deciding who would work in their buildings, to accept some teachers they did not want.

To date, these threats and sources of opposition have not caused any city to abandon its portfolio strategy. (In fact since the Great Recession began the number of major cities pursuing the strategy has doubled.) However, threats and opposition are likely to grow as the strategy becomes more prevalent. As the strategy becomes the established way of doing business, the leaders identified with it also come to own the many problems that inevitably arise in big city school systems. The portfolio strategy surely will not cause school shootings, flu epidemics, transportation breakdowns, or teacher sexual abuse scandals, but as it becomes the established formula, it will catch the blame.

Despite its surprising hardiness to date, the portfolio strategy will never be established to the point that it is immune from the effects of negligent or incompetent leadership. The strategy is only as good as the decisions made about opening, closing, and supporting schools. If top leaders try to reduce key decisions to simple administrative processes or start making political deals to exempt some schools or neighborhoods from judgment on the basis of performance, the strategy could quickly lose its legitimacy. Though the portfolio strategy is an empirical process, not a dictatorship, it cannot survive without leaders who are able to make decisions on the evidence and take the political heat. It is easy, as happened in the case of Michelle Rhee, for a flamboyant leader to dramatize and intensify conflict, to the point that reaction to her personality becomes opposition to the reform. A portfolio strategy needs a special kind of leader, a technocrat who can handle opposition. These leaders exist—Denver's Tom Boasberg, New Orleans's John White, and Hartford's Christina Kishimoto are prime examples—but they are in short supply.

> *The portfolio strategy is a process, not a dictatorship, but it can't survive without leaders who can make decisions and take the political heat.*

Why Portfolio Strategies Are Hardy

Portfolio strategies last longer and have survived leadership transitions that we and many other observers would have expected, given their complexity and tendency to stir up conflict. In retrospect, this is likely due to the following five factors.[3]

—A portfolio strategy involves a much broader set of local actors than do conventional school reform initiatives.

—Most portfolio strategies emerge from crises that change the local politics of public education, at least temporarily.

—A portfolio strategy is easier to explain to people involved in scientific professions, investment, and business than are initiatives contained within the education profession.

—Leaders of portfolio districts are more likely than conventional school superintendents to understand community politics and the challenges of political leadership.

—Districts pursuing a portfolio strategy benefit from a broad consensus among elected officials and among newer philanthropies.

Many Local Actors

A portfolio strategy involves a much broader set of local actors than do conventional school reform initiatives. School reform strategies that take the schools as they are and try to improve them by training or motivating teachers are naturally contained within the school district bureaucracy. Superintendents can explain them in public and even get financial support from businesses and foundations, but people who don't work in the schools are assigned to the cheering section. In contrast, portfolio districts seek new school providers from the private schools, youth services, and higher education communities and are open to schools' making use of community resources (such as technology-based instruction vendors and neighborhood piano teachers). Schools are also more open to employing qualified teachers who are not already part of the union bargaining unit and school leaders from private schools or other sectors. Local foundations don't just help the district; they can become engaged with particular schools (such as charters) whose work they can track closely.

Thus portfolio districts can broaden participation in the way that counts most, transforming citizens from spectators to actors. New York and New Orleans also have built on this intrinsic strength of the portfolio strategy by deliberately encouraging the creation of independent support organizations that can provide professional development, advisory, financial, and other services to schools that control their own budgets. This both strengthens the portfolio strategy by enriching the options available to schools and creates a new organized base of support in the community.[4]

School leaders are another potential source of support for portfolio districts. This is obviously the case for charter school leaders, whose powers and opportunities depend on the portfolio strategy. But it can include leaders of district-run schools that gain autonomy and aspiring leaders who, as in New York City and New Orleans, can hope to be considered for principalships as soon as they are ready regardless of seniority. In New York City, leaders of autonomous district-run schools mobilized against budget-driven proposals to force-place troubled teachers who had previously been kept in district-run rubber rooms.

In general, the decentralization of decisionmaking and the devolution of control of money—whether to schools or to independent support organizations—can help buttress a portfolio strategy. In the future, determined mayors, school boards, or other political groups might want to abandon the strategy, but to do so they will need to claw back money that had been entrusted to educators and nonprofit service organizations.

Change in the Politics of Public Education

Most portfolio strategies emerge from crises that change the local politics of public education, at least temporarily. State and mayoral takeovers bypass elected school boards, which in turn weaken the dominant actors in school board elections, teacher unions, and parents in better-off neighborhoods. As in New York and New Orleans, forces that are normally quiescent in local education politics—mayors, businesses, new school providers and other nonprofits, and philanthropies—become energized. Decisionmaking is centralized in a chief executive and bypasses the traditional processes of bargaining and consultation, which are dominated by unions and their allies (elected officials and established vendors to the school district).

These changes allow bold action, and as long as the mayor or other powerful actors remain engaged, they can survive opposition from traditionally dominant groups. This explains why portfolio strategies have survived longer than most districtwide initiatives. However, dramatic actions like mayoral takeovers are finite in duration, as was evident in Hartford when the mayor, an early portfolio strategy sponsor, was forced to resign.

In the long run, the most powerful people in the city will move on to other matters. The strategy's continuation will require establishing a long-term governance system, less open to dominance by employees and advantage-seeking parents and vendor groups.

Strategy Familiar to Other Actors

A portfolio strategy is easier to explain to people involved in scientific professions, investment, and business than are initiatives contained within the education profession. Though civic and professional leaders will often defer to superintendents who assert that some within-the-profession activity will improve all the schools (such as districtwide use of a branded professional development or instructional program), they seldom understand it. When the districtwide program does not live up to its promise, generally improving a few schools but not helping the lowest income schools—those with the highest teacher and principal turnover and worst ties to families—the reform program, and the people who brought it, are easily abandoned.

The portfolio strategy closely resembles the methods of problem solving in professional fields like medicine, engineering, and investment, where current practices are never good enough, and the best route to improvement must be discovered. In those fields it is natural to experiment with many promising options, to reject most, but to adopt the ones that work best. Professionals in these fields understand that serious trials of many approaches, including identification and abandonment of failures, are necessary. For them, a trial of multiple ideas is more sensible than a bet on a single panacea, and frequent (though not universal) failures are not discrediting. This basic understanding allows portfolio district leaders to own their failures, not hide them, and to constantly introduce new ideas without being accused of overall failure.

Thus a portfolio strategy can be stable even as it incrementally but steadily changes the mix of schools and other services it offers and simultaneously manages constant opposition. This assumes, of course, that the CEO and other district leaders are transparent and consistent about their reasons for actions, like school closings, that inconvenience some families, educators, and neighborhood leaders. It also assumes that they build in a system to evaluate their efforts.[5]

Strategy Leaders and Community Politics

Leaders of portfolio districts are more likely to understand community politics and the challenges of political leadership than conventional school superintendents. Most superintendents believe their real work is in the schools and that political campaigns, contentious forums, and involvement in lawsuits are deadweight burdens. Conventional superintendents typically work their whole careers within schools and within the public education bureaucracy. Some (like Hartford's Stephen Adamowski and Cleveland's Eric Gordon) show remarkable political skill and insight, despite the fact that these traits are not the focus of their training and experience. Moreover, big city superintendents are usually itinerants hired from other districts and even states. Few have a deep understanding of the histories or power structures—or have the opportunity to sufficiently grasp the political cultures—of the cities whose schools they lead.

In contrast, many portfolio district leaders come from professions other than education. They are experienced in politics and public sector leadership and are deeply grounded in the communities they serve. Klein, Pastorek, Bennet, Boasberg, and Duncan all fit this description, as does Mayor Jackson of Cleveland. In addition, all but Duncan are lawyers, accustomed to conflict and not intimidated by threats of lawsuits. Even those early portfolio district leaders who were not local residents, such as Paul Vallas, were from political and general government backgrounds. Thus their experiences better prepared them to deal with the broader forces that gathered in and around their portfolio reform initiatives.

As the portfolio strategy spreads to more cities, a new kind of leader appears to be emerging. These are individuals, whether career educators or people from other professions, who have worked closely with a prominent portfolio district leader, most frequently Joel Klein. Klein alumni led districts in Baltimore (Andres Alonso), Chicago (Jean-Claude Brizard), New Haven (Garth Herries), Louisiana (John White), and Newark (Cami Anderson). Now portfolio district leaders are grooming their successors and getting them appointed. In the last three years, three portfolio district leaders were succeeded by their handpicked successors (Kaya Henderson in Washington, Christina Kishimoto in Hartford, and John Deasy in Los Angeles).

Developing a bench—leaders who can step in for a city they know well and also to reliably lead a portfolio strategy a new city—is essential to the continuation of the portfolio strategy and its expansion to other cities. To date this has been done informally but with success. Further expansion may depend on more formalized recruitment, training, and on-the-job training programs. A portfolio strategy is not leader dependent in the sense that it requires unique and irreproducible skills or depends on the mystique associated with one respected person. However, as a framework for problem solving, a portfolio strategy is not a machine that can be set up and left to run automatically.

Leaders, starting with the superintendent or CEO, must constantly monitor existing and potential schools, assiduously identify opportunities for improvements, regularly inform parents and other communities of interest, and take actions (including school openings and closings) that are likely to cause conflict. Thus it seems unlikely that portfolio strategies can ever be led by individuals who have only analytical or instructional skills and who lack fine political judgment. The most important decisions involve a close balancing of benefits and costs and careful work with parents and neighbors to explain the rationales for actions and the ways children will benefit.[6]

Consensus

Finally, districts pursuing a portfolio strategy benefit from a broad consensus among elected officials at the federal and state level and among newer philanthropies, including Democrats for Education Reform and the Bill and Melinda Gates Foundation, in favor of choice, innovation, and performance-based accountability. President Barack Obama's support of charter schools, the priorities of the federal Race to the Top competition, and the performance requirements of No Child Left Behind create a friendly environment for portfolio districts, as do similar policies at the state level. Though Democrats aligned with teachers' unions often oppose the portfolio district idea, it also has many Democratic as well as Republican supporters.

Developing a "bench" of leaders is essential to sustaining a portfolio strategy.

While not all new philanthropies embrace the portfolio district idea, most of them invest in organizations that portfolio districts rely on (Teach for America, KIPP and other charter management organizations, and new sources of school and district leaders, like New Leaders for New Schools and Broad Fellows).

This general environment of acceptance has aided the growth and continuation of portfolio district strategies. However, earlier consensuses in favor of standards-based reform, mastery learning, and standard districtwide instructional frameworks have not been enough to hold those strategies in place. It is not yet clear whether political changes—including warfare between moderates of both political parties and the Tea Party—will disrupt the proportfolio consensus.

Policy and Philanthropy: Twin Pillars of the Portfolio Strategy

Throughout this book we focus on the actions of local actors, particularly school system leaders and city mayors, who have introduced and led portfolio strategies. The focus is appropriate; local actors are the ones who do the hard, everyday work. However, other actors, particularly in the state government and in philanthropies both national and local, also play indispensable roles.

State legislators and governors have supported policies—mayoral takeovers, raised charter school caps, greater hiring flexibility, and experimentation with new forms of schooling—without which local portfolio strategies would have been impossible. Philanthropies have also invested in the independent nonprofit organizations that provide needed educational and managerial support for autonomous schools.

State Legislation, a Key Enabler

It is hard to imagine a portfolio strategy being adopted or enduring for long in a state that does not allow charter schools, permit districts to use student outcomes as a factor in determining which schools to close, and allow principals to choose teachers on grounds other than seniority.

In most states with active portfolio districts, state laws have also empowered mayors or other noneducation actors to take over districts, at least temporarily, and to limit school board powers to approving or blocking initiatives taken by the mayor, CEO, or superintendent. New York State's law enabling Michael Bloomberg to take over the city's schools and Louisiana's RSD (which took over the majority of New Orleans schools in 2005 following the hurricane-caused devastation) are well known. Mayoral control laws in Washington, Cleveland, Los Angeles, Boston, Chicago, and Baltimore were on the books long before the portfolio strategy was introduced. But they provided the necessary underpinnings for the strategy once it was adopted. Similarly, takeover by a state-appointed master led to the adoption of a portfolio strategy in Oakland.[7]

These state laws were enough to support portfolio strategy launches; but are they enough to sustain the strategy once the original leaders depart or opponents gain strength? Clearly, despite strong legislative underpinnings, the portfolio strategies in Washington, New York City, and New Orleans—some of the most mature portfolio districts—have been challenged. The continuation of the strategy in New York will depend heavily on the inclinations of the next mayor, who will take office in 2014. New Orleans schools now controlled by the RSD must be returned to some form of local control by 2015. And there is reason to wonder whether the elected city or parish officials there can resist the temptation to recentralize control of jobs and money.

Can state laws go beyond enabling portfolio strategies, to make them the normal and permanent way of doing business? Examples of state laws meant to buttress portfolio strategies include Colorado's Innovation Schools Act (which allows districts not only to devolve decisions about spending, staffing, instructional methods, and time use to schools but also to monitor schools solely on performance) and Louisiana's RSD law (which created a permanent state capacity to take over and transform persistently low-performing schools).

The Colorado Innovation Schools Act—coupled with the state's charter school law, its growth-model-based accountability system, and its within- and across-district choice policies—go a long way toward supporting the indefinite continuation of its portfolio district strategy. Together, these have enabled Denver to pursue a portfolio strategy over an extended period, in the absence of a mayoral takeover or the suspension of normal school board powers and with an active teachers' union. In New Orleans the RSD works with a flexible charter school law and a well-established state performance accountability system to incentivize district leaders to transform low-performing schools so the state won't take them over. Other states, including Tennessee, Michigan, and New Jersey, have created their own analogs of Louisiana's RSD. In theory, a permanent RSD presses city and district leaders to adopt a portfolio approach for themselves. In reality, conventional districts have proven more likely to organize politically against the RSD than to imitate it.

In a recent gathering of civic and district leaders pursuing the portfolio strategy, a group discussion led to consensus on a number of state policy changes that could both enable and stabilize a portfolio strategy (box 6-1).[8] In Louisiana, state RSD officials are working to create a governance system for New Orleans schools that will be overseen by a locally elected school board but that will preserve the entrepreneurial character of the current system and continue to attract talented educators from

BOX 6-1. Possible Changes in State Policy

The following are suggestions for state policies recommended by portfolio district and local foundation leaders.

Improve data and accountability.

Free up district central-office staff from compliance requirements and management of separate funding streams.

Provide test results much faster, to support school staffing, opening, and closing decisions.

Allow districts to become all-charter districts exempt from the state education code (that is, enact a Colorado-style innovation zone that sets student outcome goals but allows experimentation with methods).

Increase district and school flexibility in teacher hiring.

Move tenure decisions from the third to the seventh year of employment.

Open up initial teacher licensure by requiring performance evidence for renewal.

Establish districts' right to dismiss teachers quickly for just cause.

Eliminate reduction in force by seniority (to protect new schools from bearing all the burden of staff layoffs).

Make schools, not the district, the employers of teachers and the bargaining unit for collective bargaining.

Fund schools based on enrollment.

Consolidate all funding programs into one pupil-based stream.

Make it possible for districts to use chartering as part of their core strategy.

Allow districts to solicit applications for charters to serve particular students and neighborhoods.

Give districts the authority to close low-performing charters operating within their boundaries.

Create an independent status for existing district-run schools that gives them charterlike freedom.

Let districts that sponsor charters get credit for their student counts.

Eliminate pension and benefit arrangements that discourage teachers from transferring to charter schools.

Eliminate caps on number of charters.

Allow one organization to run multiple schools under one charter.

Make all public schools, whether charter or district run, meet the same performance standards.

BOX 6-2.   Principles for Alternate Governance Models

The model is overseen by an elected board.

The chief executive enjoys enough independence to be effective.

The governing board and the CEO focus mainly on effective learning opportunities for children.

Schools may be run in a variety of ways (such as direct run, charter, and contract).

The playing field is level, so that schools of all types have a chance to succeed.

Students are funded equally, regardless of where they attend school.

Full public information and fair admissions processes are ensured.

Special education is provided no matter where a child goes to school.

The system seeks, attracts, and rewards the most capable people available, locally and nationwide.

The model is adaptable as needs, evidence about performance, and possibilities for instruction emerge.

Money is not tied up permanently in programs, salaries, or facilities.

Employment agreements are short term or are conditional on performance.

The model is open to virtual schooling and to new ways to use time, money, facilities, and teachers.

---

across the country. Already several alternative governance models have been proposed. Ultimately, each will be judged on how well it implements certain principles (box 6-2).[9]

The principles in box 6-2—and any governance model that puts them into practice—are sure to be controversial, as national unions and their allies press for a system that allows for a fixed set of schools and permanent employment. In Louisiana and elsewhere, the portfolio strategy's long-term stability is likely to require a similar profound rethinking of the roles and missions of local school boards and school districts.

The Importance of Philanthropy

The portfolio districts we study here all received help from philanthropies, but the amounts received differed dramatically. The most widely publicized cities—New York, Washington, Chicago, New Orleans, and Los Angeles—received millions of dollars from national and local foundations. New York and Chicago benefited from the fact that many very large national foundations are also local. Baltimore and Denver also received significant help from national foundations but depended heavily on smaller, locally based philanthropies. Hartford, Cleveland, and Cincinnati depended almost entirely on regional and local foundations.

The absolute amounts contributed are in the tens of millions of dollars a year nationwide. However, a New York University analysis of overall K–12 spending in New York City shows that philanthropy represents only a tiny fraction (less than 1 percent) of the total.[10] The tens of millions of dollars from the Gates Foundation and the Eli Broad Foundation are dwarfed by regular state and local funding in a city that spends over $24 billion a year. Federal stimulus spending in 2009 and 2010 also functioned as temporary "new money." Most of that was spent on avoiding teacher layoffs. But in cities that received i3 grants and participated in state Race to the Top grants, some federal money looked like philanthropy.

Much the same is true in the other prominent portfolio districts. Even in the smaller districts like Hartford, philanthropy represents as high a proportion of public expenditures as it does in New York. With one major exception (Washington) national foundation grants for portfolio districts supported building new capacities: new school providers and charter management organizations and new nonprofits to provide advice and assistance to charters and other autonomous schools. Gates's early grants in support of New York City's small high schools largely went to the creation of independent support networks, like New Visions. Ironically, these grants (which the Gates Foundation itself labeled failures because the new small high schools started slowly) created a support infrastructure on which the portfolio strategy later relied.

National foundations have also invested millions of dollars in New Schools for New Orleans, which then reinvested the money in charter management organizations, new school start-ups, teacher and principal recruitment, and nonprofits that sell needed services to charter schools. In general, both the national foundations and local leaders understood that philanthropy was best used for one-time investments in organizations that, once established, would be supported with state and local government money.

All the portfolio cities have benefited from national foundations' investments in Teach for America, the New Teacher Project, and New Leaders for New Schools. Chicago has also benefited from decades of investments by the MacArthur, Joyce, and Spencer foundations in new schools, community organizations, and other nonprofits that support school reform. In addition, Chicago benefits from nearly twenty years of foundation investments in the independent Consortium on Chicago Schools Research, which provides quick and credible feedback on what current reforms have and have not accomplished. Similar organizations are getting started in other localities. Washington is the only portfolio city that received multimillion-dollar grants to pay teacher salaries; this salary scale was to be available to teachers who accepted Michelle Rhee's performance-based accountability plan. In the long run, these costs are to be paid from the city's funds, based on ambitious assumptions about new management efficiencies. In the smaller cities, local foundation funds paid for consultants, for meetings to plan reform strategies, and for new central office capacities (such as strengthening data systems and charter school offices).

All of these investments helped local portfolio district leaders get started and to build capacities that probably will help sustain the strategy. However, these portfolio districts would be badly hurt by a withdrawal of philanthropic support. Only a few localities have invested in independent support organizations, and to date these are by no means able to provide all the support independent schools need and can pay for. Like all school districts, portfolio districts face pressure to spend all their public funds on direct services to students and on salaries. Capacity building always depends on philanthropy. Continued support for this function is indispensable; as the numbers of portfolio districts grow, so will the need. A shift in charitable foundation priorities, whether due to declines in stock portfolios or to new philanthropic fads, can threaten the sustainability of portfolio district strategies.

No Declaring Victory

In general, portfolio districts have tried to open enough new schools to create a record of high performance and to build support among groups not unalterably opposed to them. They have also tried to make irreversible changes—in rules, organization, funding, personnel, and interest group configurations outside the district—to make it difficult to stop the reform and bring the old system back.

Over time, portfolio school districts will continue to evolve, adopting new approaches and transitioning to new leadership. Some cities may be able to build and expand on the strategy by finding highly capable leaders who understand what has been done and will work to sustain it. Others will not. Some cities will enjoy support from citizens; in others, opponents may continually challenge the reform. As with launching the portfolio strategy, institutionalizing the reform is not only the work of school district leaders and staff. They will need allies.

The combination of technical expertise, organizational capacity, political will, and authority demanded by the reform requires not only putting routines and policies in place but also cultivating coalition partners inside and outside of the district in support of the reform. Leadership succession, the ongoing need to develop and ensure the quality of the educator workforce, the refinement and continuous improvement of management systems, the challenge of sustaining the reform in the face of tight budgets, and the potential loss of philanthropic funding are all critical elements of institutionalizing portfolio reform. As chapter 5 shows, city leaders have not made sure they have unimpeachable evidence of success, and this leaves them vulnerable. Some are also struggling with the need to close unsuccessful schools that were opened on their watch, an action that is inevitable in a continuous improvement system but one that erodes any pretentions of infallibility.

Researchers and policymakers are typically shortsighted, thinking that success or failure of a reform strategy can be seen in a few short years (such as the duration of the typical research or capacity-building grant). A study that tracks the evolution of K–12 reform in Los Angeles demonstrates the value of a longer view.[11] In the book *Learning from LA*, the authors show that reform initiatives come and go but that the school system never returns to the status quo ante. Instead, the next reform initiative builds on the one before, in part by attracting new actors and institutionalizing new capacities but also by destroying the capacities on which earlier systems depended. As they suggest, reform initiatives have a ratchet effect: even when reaction against a reform strategy takes the pressure off, the system evolves from where the just-abandoned strategy left it.

There are many reasons why this might be true of the portfolio strategy. It has engaged a broader public, created new expectations on the part of parents and educators, broken union and central office bureaucracies, and created school providers and assistance organizations that are not likely to go away. If in places like New York political opposition stops the growth of the portfolio strategy, it is likely to emerge again in more advanced form once the political cycle turns again.

CHAPTER SEVEN
A Ratchet Effect?

Andre, an elementary schoolteacher in Washington, likes the new union contract and the way teachers get observed and advised by peers. He was glad when Michelle Rhee resigned, but he wouldn't want to roll back anything she accomplished—even though some of his colleagues hate everything done under Rhee and Mayor Adrian Fenty and want to go back to the old system, where there was not so much testing and teachers did not have to worry about their jobs.

Andre hopes the district will slow down the introduction of "reform" ideas, but he says that if everything went back to the old way he would leave Washington and go some place where a dedicated teacher has a chance to succeed. He hopes his union leaders and the neighborhood activists he knows will stop fighting against what is now in place—that they will use it, not tear it down.

Readers will not have missed the fact that city and school district leaders who introduce portfolio strategies do so with different degrees of skill, different degrees of respect for others' views, and a different taste for confrontation. We do not claim that the conflicts observed in the cities we studied are all inevitable (for example, in Washington, where the school chancellor appeared on a national magazine cover with a broom, symbolizing her intent to clean house with teachers). But it is evident that portfolio strategies generate conflict even when led with tact and open-mindedness.

As this is written the portfolio strategy is continuing in the cities that were first to adopt it and is being taken up by additional cities. However, given the conflict they engender, local portfolio strategies are likely always to have strong opposition and to depend on the commitment of a few key individuals—a mayor, the swing voter on a divided school board, a superintendent, a union leader.

District leadership teams are also small and subject to abrupt changes, as individuals retire, return to their permanent careers, or take education leadership jobs in other cities. New York City, which has exported people who became portfolio leaders in New Orleans, Baltimore, Rochester, Chicago, Newark, and New Haven, might soon suffer from the loss of leadership talent. Rochester's commitment to the portfolio strategy did not survive Jean-Claude Brizard's departure for Chicago, but Chicago's is likely to continue despite his resignation.

If portfolio strategies stall out in some cities, will the old system come fully back? Based on what we have seen, the answer is probably no. School leaders have learned to appreciate controlling their budgets and hiring decisions and will resist giving them back. Parents, including those from low-income areas who did not have good options before and those from higher income areas, who are swelling enrollment in many cities, will be reluctant to give up their choices. New teachers—including not only career switchers but also newcomers recruited from Teach for America and well-organized dissident groups within local teachers' unions—might be outnumbered for a while, but they won't go away.

The portfolio strategy has also brought people and organizations that were once on the sidelines into public education. These include the colleges, universities, businesses, and nonprofits that have become involved as school operators and service providers; in addition, new nonprofits have formed to manage schools and provide assistance that was once available only from the district central office. If school district leadership discouraged such organizations from involvement in public education, the existing entities could easily go back to their previous work. However, the new organizations—charter schools, charter management organizations, service providers, and local boards composed of active and prominent citizens—might object, since they have more to lose. And the leaders who want to exclude them would be pressed to explain how the schools would be better off without the resources these organizations bring.

Some events could destroy a city's portfolio initiative: a legislature might repeal its charter school law and forbid the practice of relying on nonprofits to provide support services. District leaders might fall back on old habits of central control and slowly erode schools' control over hiring and budgets.[1] Readers can make their judgments about how likely these things are to happen. If they don't happen, district leaders who want to back away from the portfolio strategy will be hard pressed to exclude these entities and their resources entirely. The result will be that the foundational elements of the portfolio strategy are likely to remain even in districts that have stopped actively pursuing it.

A more realistic possibility in some cities is stalemate, with opponents unable to tear down what has been built under the portfolio strategy but with supporters unable to advance it. This seems possible, and it could happen almost anywhere as the result of a mayoral or school board election. However, stalemates themselves might not last, if city leaders once again become concerned that weaknesses in the public education system are threatening the city's growth and prosperity. The bottom line is that portfolio strategies, once started, might be halted—but they probably can't be rooted out.

The portfolio strategy incorporates many reform ideas that are often presented as stand-alone panaceas (such as school choice and performance-based accountability) but treats them as mutually reinforcing parts of a broader strategy. It attracts supporters and opponents on both the left and right.

Some progressives fear that the portfolio strategy will inject competition into a function (schooling) that they think should be communitarian; however, other progressives value it as a way to open up options for the poor. Some conservatives favor the portfolio strategy as a way to ensure that schools live and die on the basis of performance; others fear that district-managed portfolios will blunt the movement for more radical reforms, such as unregulated school vouchers.

Even during the current recession, cuts in public spending have broken down political and ideological barriers and made productivity and efficiency a less ideological issue. This extends to broadened support for opening up the teaching profession to people from other professions and to experimentation with technology to maintain the quality of instruction even while funding falls. The portfolio strategy is a plausible settling point between purely market and purely governmental solutions.[2] That, more than the current state of play in any locality, is likely to guarantee that the idea will endure and spread.

Conflict is proof neither of the failure nor of the success of a school reform strategy. Conflict only means that issues once considered settled are up again for discussion. In all likelihood, the more significant the reform—or more accurately, the less incremental the change on who benefits and to what degree—the more overt the conflict in its implementation.

Notes

Chapter 1

1. Frederick M. Hess, *Spinning Wheels: The Politics of Urban School Reform* (Brookings, 1998).

Chapter 2

1. Portfolio districts in 2012: Austin, Baltimore, Boston, Central Falls (Rhode Island), Chicago, Cincinnati, Clark County (Las Vegas), Cleveland, Denver, Detroit, Washington, Hartford, Indianapolis, Jefferson Parish (Louisiana), Los Angeles, Milwaukee, Minneapolis, Nashville, New Haven, New York City, Oakland, Philadelphia, Louisiana Recovery School District, Rochester, N.Y., Sacramento, Spring Branch (Texas), and Tennessee Achievement School District.

2. Elise Huggins, with Mary Beth Celio, "Closing the Achievement Gap in Washington State: Holding Schools Accountable for Equity" (Seattle: Center on Reinventing Public Education, 2005).

3. Ibid.

4. Paul E. Peterson and others, "Are US Students Ready to Compete?" *Education Next* (2010).

5. The concept of continuous quality improvement was developed by W. Edwards Deming, who famously applied it to Japanese industry starting in the 1950s. It has since been applied to almost every other field of work.

6. Robin J. Lake and Betheny Gross, "New York City's iZone" (Seattle: Center on Reinventing Public Education, 2011).

7. See http://gothamschools.org/2009/02/10/mayor-beats-his-own-deadline-to-open-100-charter-schools.

8. "A Growing Movement: America's Largest Charter School Communities" (Washington: National Alliance for Public Charter Schools, 2011).

9. For more on New York City's extensive subportfolio of multiple pathways to graduation, see www.nyc.gov/html/ceo/downloads/pdf/appendixb_multiplepathways.pdf.

10. Arthur Levine, "Education School Leaders" (Washington: Education Schools Project, 2005).

11. Former New Orleans teachers who were not hired back have sued for damages. See *Eddy Oliver, Oscarlene Nixon, and Mildred Goodwin* vs. *Orleans Parish School Board.*

12. Christine Campbell and Michael DeArmond, "Talent Management in Portfolio School Districts" (Seattle: Center on Reinventing Public Education, 2010).

13. Teacher certification requirements determine who can work in a classroom. Some of these rules are state law, while others are set by local school boards. They include college completion, enrollment or completion in a teacher preparation program, and passing scores on state teacher exams.

14. Denver's PROCOMP teacher salary plan is well documented in Phil Gonring, Paul Teske, and Brad Jupp, *Pay-for-Performance Teacher Compensation: An Inside View of Denver's ProComp Plan* (Harvard Education Press, 2007). Though Denver leaders have not aggressively used PROCOMP as a recruiting tool, they report increased success in retaining their most talented new teachers.

15. See http://wamu.org/news/11/09/13/more_dcps_teachers_accepting_bonuses. Teachers receiving a rating of "highly effective" for two years in a row can also receive a boost in their base salary, up to an equivalent of five extra years of seniority. In 2011, 292 teachers earned this service credit.

16. For a more elaborate treatment of these ideas, see Paul T. Hill and Robin J. Lake, "Performance Management in Portfolio School Districts" (Seattle: Center on Reinventing Public Education, 2009).

17. Samuel R. Sperry, "Better Schools through Better Politics: The Human Side of Portfolio School District Reform" (Seattle: Center on Reinventing Public Education, 2012).

18. Sharon Otterman and Allison Kpicki, "New Yorkers Say Mayor Has Not Improved Schools," *New York Times*, September 6, 2011.

19. Sperry, Better Schools through Better Politics.

Chapter 3

1. Charles Kerchner and colleagues identify six steps leading to profound change in public school districts: 1. The old institution is discredited and delegitimized. 2. Significant portions of its most vocal clients leave the system. 3. The functions of the system are removed (hollowed out) and given to other levels of government. 4. There are frantic efforts at reform and auditioning new ideas. 5. There is a defining crisis or a recognized end to a long-term crisis and uncertainty. 6. The new institution is operationally recognized, and someone writes a text about how it should operate. See Charles T. Kerchner and others, *Learning from L.A.: Institutional Change in American Public Education* (Harvard Education Press, 2008), p. 4.

2. Ibid.

3. See Paul T. Hill, "Re-Creating Public Education in New Orleans," *Education Week*, September 21, 2005.

4. Paul T. Hill, Christine Campbell, and James Harvey, *It Takes a City: Getting Serious about Urban School Reform* (Brookings, 2000); Hill, "Re-Creating Public Education in New Orleans"; Paul Hill and Jane Hannaway, "The Future of Public Education in New Orleans," in *After Katrina: Rebuilding Equity and Opportunity into the New New Orleans*, edited by Margery Austin Turner and Sheila R. Zedlewski (Washington: Urban Institute, 2006).

5. Jennifer O'Day, Catherine S. Bitter, and Louis M. Gomez, eds., *Education Reform in New York City: Ambitious Change in the Most Complex School System* (Harvard Education Press, 2011).

6. Nancy Mitchell and Burt Hubbard, "Leaving to Learn," *Rocky Mountain News,* April 16, 2007.

7. Superintendent Michael Bennet and the Denver School Board, "A Vision for a 21st Century School District," *Rocky Mountain News,* April 25, 2007.

8. For a detailed account of ProComp, see Phil Gonring, Paul Teske, and Brad Jupp, *Pay-for-Performance Teacher Compensation: An Inside View of Denver's Pro-Comp Plan* (Harvard Education Press, 2007).

9. For an example of the kinds of displays possible under Denver's data system, see http://testing.dpsk12.org/fusioncharts/spf/default.asp?chart=growthstatus_frl_es.

10. Democratic legislator Peter Groff introduced the Innovation Schools Act of 2008 (www.cde.state.co.us/cdedocs/OPP/SB130Statute.pdf).

11. Personal communication between Michael Bennet and Paul Hill, September 2006.

12. Leanne Stiefel and Amy Ellen Schwartz, "Financing K–12 Education in the Bloomberg Years, 2002–2008," in *Education Reform in New York City*, edited by O'Day, Bitter, and Gomez, pp. 75–83.

13. On the Cleveland Plan, see www.gcpartnership.com/Talent/Primary-and-Secondary-Education/The-Cleveland-Plan.aspx.

Chapter 4

1. Public Agenda, "An Assessment of Survey Data on Attitudes about Teaching, Including the Views of Parents, Administrators, Teachers, and the General Public," 2003 (http://publicagenda.org/pages/attitudes-about-teaching).

2. See http://www.gallup.com/poll/122504/Public-Says-Better-Teachers-Key-Improved-Education.aspx.

3. Private schools, which are voluntary but depend on tuition payments, face similar if not as complex challenges.

4. Disclosure: The senior author was an expert witness for the defense in the Louisiana case *Eddy Oliver et al.* v. *New Orleans Parish School Board*, a class action suit brought by former New Orleans teachers.

5. See, for example, Fred M. Newman and others, "School Instructional Program Coherence: Benefits and Challenges" (Consortium on Chicago Schools Research, 2001).

6. Quotations from Sharon Otterman, "Choir Academy of Harlem Takes Advantage of Reprieve," *New York Times,* December 7, 2010.

7. See Leanna Stiefel and Amy Schwartz, "Financing K–12 Education in the Bloomberg Years," in *Education Reform in New York City: Ambitious Change in the Nation's Most Complex School System,* edited by Jennifer A. O'Day, Catherine S. Bitter, and Louis M. Gomez (Harvard Education Press, 2011), pp. 55–86.

8. However, these investments, though large in absolute dollars, were very small compared to the districts' operational funding. In New York, philanthropy amounted to less than 2 percent of all funding, which totals nearly $20 billion a year. This is not a particularly large share compared to other metropolitan districts. The philanthropic share of all spending is also not high relative to historic patterns of contribution in Denver or Chicago. It is not clear whether Mark Zuckerberg's promised $100 million investment in Newark schools will put that city's philanthropic funding at a higher level than that of other districts. Much depends on how quickly that money is made available, for what, and whether existing sources of private money dry up.

9. Each year teachers advance to the next salary step in the lane they are in, until they reach the maximum step.

10. Stephen Brill, "The Rubber Room: The Battle over New York City's Worst Teachers," *New Yorker,* August 31, 2009.

11. M. Goertz, S. Loeb, and J. Wyckoff, "Recruiting, Evaluating, and Retaining Teachers: The Children-First Strategy to Improve New York City's Teachers," in *Education Report in New York City,* edited by O'Day, Bitter, and Gomez, pp. 157–77.

12. See, for example, Sam Dillon, "A Tentative Contract Deal for Washington Teachers," *New York Times,* April 7, 2010. See also Sam Dillon, "In Washington, Large Rewards in Teacher Pay," *New York Times,* December 31, 2011.

13. For these various references, see David Menefee-Libey, "Neoliberal School Reform in Chicago?" in *Between Public and Private: Politics, Governance, and the New Portfolio Models for Urban School Reform,* edited by Katrina E. Bulkley, Jeffrey R. Henig, and Henry Levin (Harvard Education Press, 2010), pp. 55–90; Dorothy Shipps, *School Reform, Corporate Style, Chicago 1880–2000* (University of Kansas Press, 2006); Naomi Klein, "The Shock Doctrine in Action in New Orleans," *Huffington Post,* December 21, 2007 (www.huffingtonpost.com/naomi-klein/the-shock-doctrine-in-act_b_77886.html). See also Naomi Klein, *The Shock Doctrine: The Rise of Disaster Capitalism* (New York: Henry Holt, 2007).

14. Clarence Stone, "Urban Regimes and the Capacity to Govern," Journal of Urban Affairs 15, no. 1 (1993): 1–28.

15. Charles F. Sabel, "A Quiet Revolution of Democratic Governance: Towards Democratic Experimentalism," in *Organisation for Economic Cooperation and Development: Governance in the 21st Century* (Paris: OECD, 2001), pp. 121–49.

16. For more on this point, see Samuel R. Sperry, "Better Schools through Better Politics" (Seattle: Center on Reinventing Public Education, 2012).

Chapter 5

1. Clara Hemphill and Kim Nauer, "The New Marketplace: How Small-School Reforms and School Choice Have Reshaped New York City's High Schools" (Center for New York City Affairs, 2009).

2. Scott S. Cowen Institute for Public Education Initiatives, "The State of Public Education in New Orleans," 2012 Report (Tulane), pp. 26–31.

3. A+ Denver, "Denver School Performance by School Board Member Districts: Results and Trends" (Citizens for Denver Schools, 2012). See also A+ Denver, "Student Achievement in Denver: The Impact of Charter Schools" (Citizens for Denver Schools, 2012).

4. Jennifer Settle and others, "The Transformation of a School System: Principal, Teacher, and Parent Perceptions of Charter and Traditional Schools in Post-Katrina New Orleans" (Santa Monica, Calif.: Rand, 2011).

5. Margaret Raymond and others, "Charter School Performance in New York City" (Stanford, Calif.: CREDO, 2010).

6. Stuart Luppescu and others, "Trends in Chicago's Schools across Three Eras of Reform" (Consortium on Chicago Schools Research, 2011).

7. The sociologist Aaron Pallas provides examples of use of such comparisons to debunk rather than validate the effectiveness of a portfolio district (http://eyeoned.org/content/joel-klein-vs-the-so-called-apologists-for-the-failed-status-quo_237/?utm). For New Orleans, see also Charles Hatfield, "Have RSD Schools Really Improved Significantly since 2005?" April 2011 (www.researchonreforms.org).

8. For more on the validity of different methods of judging school effects, see Charter School Achievement Consensus Panel, "Key Issues in Studying Charter Schools and Achievement: A Review and Suggestions for National Guidelines" (Seattle: Center on Reinventing Public Education, 2006).

9. Howard S. Bloom and others, "Transforming the High School Experience: How New York City's New Small Schools Are Boosting Student Achievement and Graduation Rates" (New York: MDRC, 2010).

10. Ibid.

11. Howard S. Bloom and Rebecca Unterman, "Sustained Positive Effects on Graduation Rates Produced by New York City's Small Public High Schools of Choice" (New York: MDRC, 2012).

12. Caroline Hoxby and others, "How New York City's Charter Schools Affect Achievement" (New York City Charter Schools Evaluation Project, 2009).

13. Margaret Raymond and others, "Charter School Performance in New York City" (Stanford, Calif.: CREDO, 2010).

14. Rachel Cole, James J. Kemple, and Micha D. Segeritz, "Assessing the Early Impact of School of One: Evidence from Three School-wide Pilots" (Research Alliance for New York City Schools, 2012).

15. "Charter School Performance in Louisiana" (Stanford, Calif.: CREDO, 2009).

16. Kevin Booker and others, "Achievement and Attainment in Chicago Charter Schools" (Santa Monica, Calif.: Rand, 2009).

17. Lauren Cassidy and others, "High School Reform in Chicago Public Schools: Renaissance 2010" (Menlo Park, Calif.: SRI, 2009).

18. "NYC High School Students Call for Real School Transformation, Not School Closings" (New York: Urban Youth Collaborative, 2011); Michele Cahill, "School System Designs to Increase Graduation Rates and Lift Student Performance," paper prepared for Asia Pacific Leaders Forum on Secondary Education, Carnegie Corporation, 2008.

19. New York City Department of Education, "Four Year Graduation Rate Rises as Dropout Rate Falls in Schools as They Are Phased Out," Powerpoint presented to the New York City Council, January 2011.

20. M. de la Torre and J. Gwynne, "When Schools Close: Effects on Displaced Students in Chicago" (Consortium on Chicago School Research, 2009).

21. John Engberg and others, "Closing Schools in a Shrinking District: Do Student Outcomes Depend on Which Schools Are Closed?" *Journal of Urban Economics* 71, no. 2 (2012): 189–203.

22. Luppescu and others, "Trends in Chicago's Schools across Three Eras of Reform."

23. Scott S. Cowen Institute, "The State of Public Education in New Orleans."

24. Settle and others, "The Transformation of a School System."

25. M. Goertz, S. Loeb, and J. Wyckoff, "Recruiting, Evaluation, and Retaining Teachers: The Children First Strategy to Improve New York City's Teachers," in *Education Reform in New York City: Ambitious Change in the Nation's Most Complex School System,* edited by Jennifer A. O'Day, Catherine S. Bitter, and Louis M. Gomez (Harvard Education Press: 2011), pp. 157–77.

26. Sean Corcoran, Amy Ellen Schwartz, and Meryle Weinstein, "The New York City Aspiring Principal Program: A School-Level Analysis" (http://steinhardt.nyu.edu/scmsAdmin/uploads/003/852/APP.pdf).

27. Damon Clark, Paco Martorell, and Jonah Rockoff, "School Principals and Performance," Working Paper 38 (Washington: CALDER, 2009).

28. William H. Marinell, "A Descriptive Analysis of Teacher Turnover in New York City's Middle Schools" (Research Alliance for New York City Schools, 2011).

29. State of Louisiana Board of Regents (http://regents.louisiana.gov/assets/media/2011/RegentsRecsept11FINAL.pdf).

Chapter 6

1. Frederick M. Hess, *Spinning Wheels: The Politics of Urban School Reform* (Brookings, 1998).

2. At the time of this writing, it is too soon to assess the consequences of the September 2012 teachers strike on Chicago's reform.

3. For an earlier analysis that makes some related points, see Jeffrey Hening and Katrina Bulkley, "Where Public Meets Private: Looking Forward," in *Politics, Governance, and the New Portfolio Models for Urban School Reform,* edited by Katrina E. Bulkley, Jeffrey R. Henig, and Henry M. Levin (Harvard Education Press, 2010), pp. 323–40.

4. In both cities, groups that had been vendors to the central office but lost business when spending decisions were devolved to schools became critics of the reform, partly offsetting political gains from the "new support organizations" strategy.

5. On how portfolio district leaders can minimize collateral damage and ensure that important decisions are credible, see Samuel R. Sperry, "Better Schools through Better Politics: The Human Side of Portfolio School District Reform" (Seattle: Center on Reinventing Public Education, 2012).

6. Ibid.

7. Oakland let elements of the portfolio strategy languish after the departure of the state-appointed administrator, Randy Ward, but has recommitted to the core portfolio ideas under the current superintendent, Tony Smith.

8. This occurred in an informal meeting of the Portfolio District Network, a gathering of district, municipal, and foundation leaders from thirty cities that seeks to implement elements of the portfolio strategy, and was recorded by the senior author. For more information on the network, see www.crpe.org/portfolio/districts.

9. For more on these principles and their implications, see Paul T. Hill, "Picturing a Different Governance Structure," in *Rethinking Education Governance for the New Century*, edited by Patrick McGuinn and Paul Manna, (Brookings, 2012).

10. Leana Steifel and Amy Schwartz, "Financing K-12 Education in the Bloomberg Years," in *Education Reform in New York City: Ambitious Change in the Nation's Most Complex School System,* edited by Jennifer A. O'Day, Catherine S. Bitter, and Louis M. Gomez (Harvard Education Press, 2011), pp. 55–86.

11. Charles T. Kerchner, David Menefee-Libey, and Laura Mulfinger, *Learning from LA: Institutional Change in American Public Education* (Harvard Education Press, 2008).

Chapter 7

1. Baltimore has created new incentives for schools to use central district services, but to this point schools are still free to buy from independent vendors. Sarah Yatsko, "Baltimore and the Portfolio School District Strategy" (Seattle: Center on Reinventing Public Education, 2012).

2. Terry M. Moe and Paul T. Hill, "Moving to a Mixed Model: Without an Appropriate Role for the Market, the Education Sector Will Stagnate," in *The Futures of School Reform*, edited by Jal Mehta, Robert B. Schwartz, and Frederick M. Hess (Harvard Education Press, 2012).

Index

Abercrombie, Willie (student), 81
Accountability: managing the school portfolio, 37; measuring performance, 34–37; performance-based accountability, 6, 15, 16–17, 33–38; school closures, 37–38
Achievement First (Hartford), 29, 32
Achievement School District. *See* Tennessee
Adamowski, Stephen (superintendent; Hartford), 8, 40, 43, 45, 62, 104
African Americans, 12, 28, 51, 72, 97, 99
Alonso, Andres (district leader; Baltimore), 40, 43, 45, 49–50, 63–64
Anderson, Cami (superintendent; Newark), 111
Anne E. Casey Foundation, 6
A+ Denver, 53, 94–95
Atlanta (Ga.), 106

Baltimore (Md.): adoption of portfolio strategy in, 43, 46, 63–64; central offices in, 28, 31; mayoral control law in, 113; new schools in, 33; performance gains in, 19; precursors to adoption of portfolio strategy in,

44; support for schools in, 117; teachers in, 22, 86. *See also* Alonso, Andres
Baton Rouge (La.), 10
Bennet, Michael (superintendent; Denver), 7, 8, 40, 52–61, 76, 104, 111
Bill and Melinda Gates Foundation, 56, 61, 62, 112, 117
Black, Cathie (successor to Joel Klein; New York City), 8, 77, 103
Blanco, Kathleen (governor, Louisiana), 10
Bloomberg, Michael (mayor, New York City), 32, 39, 43, 47, 87b, 103
Boasberg, Tom (deputy superintendent, Denver), 7, 40, 55–57, 58, 60, 104, 107, 111
Boston, 37, 113
Boys Choir of Harlem, 81
Brizard, Jean-Claude (Chicago Schools CEO), 33, 43, 45, 64, 104, 111, 122
Business theory of decentralization, 59–61

Cahill, Michele (senior counselor, New York City), 50

133